IN PURSUIT OF EXCELLENCE

Competitive sport today is about winning and training to win. Many athletes are professionals with careers managed by teams of specialist staff working towards the ultimate goal of world-class, medal-winning performances.

This accessible text offers students a comprehensive introduction to the phenomenon of the pursuit of excellence in sport, covering the key issues and talking points, including:

■ The history and tradition of sporting excellence
■ Comparisons of elite high-performance sport programmes in Australia, the USA, East Germany and France
■ The historical, social, political and economic impacts of sporting excellence in the UK
■ Current issues and debates, including drugs in sport
■ The future for high-performance sport.

With a clear framework for understanding and exploring key issues, questions for discussion, websites and suggestions for further reading, *In Pursuit of Excellence* is an ideal introduction for AS, A level and undergraduate students.

Michael Hill is Chief Examiner for AS and A Level PE at Edexcel, and Director of Physical and Leisure Education at the City of Stoke-on-Trent Sixth Form College.

STUDENT SPORT STUDIES
Series Editors: J. A. Mangan and Frank Galligan

This is a new series specifically for school, college and university students, written clearly and concisely by expert teachers. The series covers a range of relevant topics for those studying physical education, sports studies, leisure and recreation studies and related courses. Each volume is purposefully prepared for students facing specific course syllabuses and examinations and is sharply focused and written in plain English. The series is in response to repeated requests from students and teachers for accessible books concentrating on courses and examinations.

Frank Galligan
J. A. Mangan

IN PURSUIT OF EXCELLENCE

A student guide to elite sports development

MICHAEL HILL

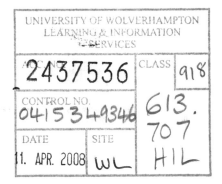
 Routledge
Taylor & Francis Group

LONDON AND NEW YORK

First published 2007
by Routledge
2 Park Square, Milton Park, Abingdon, Oxon OX14 4RN

Simultaneously published in the USA and Canada
by Routledge
270 Madison Ave, New York, NY 10016

Routledge is an imprint of the Taylor & Francis Group, an informa business

Typeset in Mixage
by Keystroke, 28 High Street, Tettenhall, Wolverhampton
Printed and bound in Great Britain
by TJ International Ltd, Padstow, Cornwall

British Library Cataloguing in Publication Data
A catalogue record for this book is available from the British Library

Library of Congress Cataloging in Publication Data
Hill, Michael, 1966–
  In pursuit of excellence : a student guide to sports development /
Michael Hill.
    p. cm. – (Student sport studies)
  Includes bibliographical references and index.
  ISBN-13: 978–0–415–34934–5 (hardback)
  ISBN-13: 978–0–415–42354–0 (pbk.)
  ISBN-10: 0–415–34934–6 (hardback)
  ISBN-10: 0–415–42354–6 (pbk.)
1. Physical education and training–Study and teaching–History.
2. Physical education and training–Study and teaching–Case studies.
3. Sports–Study and teaching–History. 4. Sports–Study and
teaching–History–Case Studies. I. Title.
  GV361.H48 2007
  613.707–dc22
                                      2006029365

ISBN10: 0–415–34934–6 (hbk)
ISBN10: 0–415–42354–6 (pbk)
ISBN10: 0–203–69540–2 (ebk)

ISBN13: 978–0–415–34934–5 (hbk)
ISBN13: 978–0–415–42354–0 (pbk)
ISBN13: 978–0–203–69540–1 (ebk)

CONTENTS

ILLUSTRATIONS

Figures

Tables

Plates

Boxes

INTRODUCTION

The aim of this book is to attempt to bring together a number of topics focusing on the diverse subject of excellence in the study of sport and recreation in society. As a contemporary issue, it is often difficult to keep abreast of the variety of programmes and cultural influences that affect the pursuit of excellence in global sport.

Students and teachers preparing for AS- and A-level and BTEC qualifications will also find the book useful in tracking both the historical background of the pursuit of excellence and the ways in which different cultures have developed elite sports programmes. Although most of the major course texts cover this area, constraints of space often dictate that the concept of excellence and its many associated issues are not fully covered. It is intended that this text will go some way to addressing this shortcoming.

This is also a common area of study for many students following undergraduate programmes in physical education, sports studies and related areas. There are few publications focusing on a comparison of systems of sports excellence available at the introductory level and particularly few providing a review of the situation in the United Kingdom (UK). For those researching or undertaking a more advanced study into excellence in sport, it is hoped that the references, web sites and suggestions for further reading will provide useful avenues for exploration.

A number of questions are given at the end of each chapter. These are simply discussion points that teachers or lecturers may wish to use in order to stimulate debate or for use by students when preparing for assessment in this area of study.

As is the case with many printed resources, keeping up to date with common issues requires some considerable degree of vigilance and is, of necessity, an ongoing process. The purpose of this text, whilst it is up to date at the time of publication, is to introduce, organise and explain the philosophies born out of cultural and political diversity that have shaped a range of approaches to the pursuit of excellence in global sport. It is hoped that readers will use the web links suggested and those provided by agencies such as UK Sport and the English Institute of Sport, as well as referring to new literature as it becomes available.

chapter one

SPORTING EXCELLENCE
The concept

We are all 'naturals' in one way: endowed with some capacity for a sporting activity. Yet, in another way, none of us is natural. Some more than others may possess great mechanical efficiency and skill in performing certain tasks and may even refine these to the point where their expertise appears effortless; so effortless in fact that it appears to be the product of a gift.

Cashmore (2005)

Participation

The pattern of sports participation can be represented by a pyramid shape (see Figure 1.1), with the majority of performers near the bottom (or what is often referred to as the grass-roots level). At this level, schoolchildren and those playing sport as a hobby or social activity participate purely for the enjoyment it brings.

Higher up the pyramid, performers are more skilful and determined so that at approximately the halfway point we find performers training and competing on a regular/weekly basis. At or very near the top of the pyramid are the elite or high-level performers who are totally committed to sport, often as a career, although not all of them may be professionals.

These elite groups contain those individuals with a special ability in sport that transcends the norm. They have reached, or are on the verge of reaching, the pinnacle of performance in their sport and are likely to be competing at national and international level.

The term 'excellence in sport' does, therefore, tend to be associated with this elite group of performers at the top of the sports pyramid. Much of the content of

3

Excellence
National and publicly
recognised standards of
performance

Performance
Higher
club/regional sport

Participation
Leisure-time sport
– local clubs

Foundation
Grass-roots – school age
and recreational participants

FIGURE 1.1
The sports-participation
pyramid.

the following chapters will concentrate on this group, although it is important
to recognise that excellence in sport for many may not occur at this highly
accomplished level.

There are actually two ways of defining sports excellence:

- elite performers/groups;
- those who achieve their own optimum performance at whatever level.

The elite model

This model refers to situations where the best performers are selected, often at
the expense of those who might normally be found in the lower echelons of the
sporting pyramid. All the available (and often limited) resources and support may
be targeted on a few talented athletes.

Such an approach is often found in emerging cultures where the need to gain
world recognition in sport is very important as a step towards national recognition (nation-building). Such countries possess limited resources, and the elite
model presents the most cost-effective way of creating winners.

The best example of a country that has successfully used this approach is the
former German Democratic Republic (East Germany), which, with a relatively
small population of 16 million people, managed to achieve phenomenal success
in global sport, especially in summer and winter Olympiads.

The East German state saw sport as an important element of its foreign policy, showing off the health and patriotism of its population to the rest of the world. East German children who were found to have natural ability were taken to special schools when very young and trained intensively, often with more systematic preparation and well-concealed use of drugs than was possible in the West.

The advantage of this elite selection process was that it produced results very quickly because it concentrated resources on those who had sporting potential. It was more economical than the comparatively haphazard selection processes then common in much of Western Europe. It produced outstanding performers, coaches and facilities and led to the development of considerable research and experimentation in terms of sports science.

Most countries now recognise that this is most effective way of producing the level of sporting success that will put them into the global 'sporting shop window'.

Undesirable outcomes

Some of the undesirable outcomes of this approach include an increasingly common tacit acceptance that if a system requires winners then the traditional sporting ethics of fair play and abiding by written and unwritten rules must be cast aside.

Issues such as drug abuse, violence and other forms of cheating become enmeshed in sport, and the intervention of states and governments in elite sports policy has simply hastened the unavoidable involvement of politics in sport.

It is important to note that although the terms 'elitism' and 'sports excellence' are often used to mean the same thing, the concept of elitism in certain contexts may differ markedly from genuinely identified sports excellence. The *Oxford Dictionary of Sports Science and Medicine* (1998) defines elitism as, 'the restriction of an activity to a privileged group. Some sports clubs restrict access on the basis of social characteristics and not athletic ability. Such elitism has resulted in the sports being associated with certain social classes and social statuses'.

It is therefore important to recognise that although elite sport excludes by definition all those whose level of sporting ability is less than excellent, there are many other less acceptable criteria that may also limit or prevent selection and participation.

The optimum performance model

This model suggests that excellence at a personal level should be the target of every individual within the sports-participation pyramid. The system acknowledges that each person has a sporting potential, and it is the objective of the system to allow all to achieve this potential, which may or may not reach the zenith of elite performance in any given activity.

Excellence in sport is often considered to be a valuable personal goal which requires that each individual should aim to achieve his or her personal best. The difficulty here lies in the fact that this is often less easily achievable in reality than it is in theory. In most circumstances, it would be very difficult to provide the facilities and resources required, even if individuals *could* be compelled to have this as their aim.

It has been suggested that the pursuit of excellence is encouraged in some cultures for a number of beneficial reasons:

- Sport can bring about a change in lifestyles that have often become increasingly sedentary and controlled.
- Curiosity about individual and human potential often means that sport is referred to as 'the last frontier'.
- Sport can provide alternative employment with the added attraction of high social status if high-level success is achieved.
- Sport can give individuals a high sense of self-esteem and a feeling of quality or worth in their lives.
- Sporting success can boost national pride and morale and accrue economic benefits.
- Mass populations can be entertained in socially accepted activities.
- The base of the participation pyramid can be expanded by increasing the numbers of those participating in sport.

Economics and excellence

Elite sports programmes are, by their nature, very costly to provide.

Modern elite performers require:

- state-of-the-art training facilities;
- highly specialised diets;
- access to high-quality coaching;

6

- high-quality sports-science support;
- the most up-to-date clothing and equipment.

The world's most successful athletes now attract huge sums in sponsorship, prize money and media contracts, but in order to reach the top in most global sports, nearly all performers will, at some point, require some form of funding, which, in an increasing number of cases is provided directly or indirectly by the state.

As previously mentioned, there are a considerable number of benefits which can accrue from success in international sport, and many state governments now recognise the potential of supporting a small number of elite athletes and their coaching and training programmes. Governments tend to support the elite model referred to above, and these tend to be emergent/younger nations.

In Australia, for example, a series of disappointing results in international sporting competitions culminating in a very poor display at the Montreal Olympic Games in 1976 led to a government review of that country's sporting infrastructure. The review resulted in the establishment of the Australian Institute of Sport (AIS) at the head of a comprehensive elite sports model funded mainly through the federal government.

Despite being one of the world's poorest nations, most of Kenya's sporting success in the twentieth century came in the field of long-distance running (see Plate 1.1).

From 1960 onwards, Kenya's male athletes dominated both Olympic and World Championship finals. Much of the support for these athletes came from the government through facilities provided via the country's armed forces.

This rise in sporting success coincided with the emergence of a newly independent Kenya, and the country's sporting successes quickly gained much international recognition. Not resting on its laurels, the Kenyan government has broadened its focus in terms of funding and programmes of sport and opened the Kenya National Sports Institute at Kasarani in 1987.

However, the severe economic constraints of the 1990s forced the government to cut its funding of sport, with the result that facilities across Kenya deteriorated. The plight of the country's sports institute worsened when a national league soccer match between AFC Leopards and Gor Mahia ended in a riot, with fans from both sides ripping out virtually all of the seats in the central stadium.

In July 2003, a deal was announced between the Kenyan and Chinese governments, with the latter offering to refurbish the whole complex at a cost of around 50 million dollars.

PLATE 1.1 Kenya can rightly claim to be the world leader in middle- and long-distance running.

Photo: Yannis Pitsiladis.

Broadening the base

In the USA and UK, there has, for the past several decades, been a gradually more inclusive approach to programmes of excellence, with a growing emphasis on offering the opportunity to achieve excellence in sport to an increasingly large number of people.

In the USA, the education system has been the key element in nurturing male – and more recently female – elite performers. Hemery (1991) states that the majority of US colleges and universities partially or wholly subsidise the cost of education for their better sportsmen and women.

With the economic advantages that the US 'superpower' enjoys, this support is now available to thousands of athletes. University teams are provided with world-class facilities, equipment and professional coaching. Travel costs are underwritten in order to allow university teams to participate fully in local, regional and national competitions.

Those who continue and progress in their chosen sport are selected from college teams onto Olympic squads or are drafted into the professional leagues. However, there is practically no club system, such as that in the UK, to which sportsmen and women can transfer after their time at university. Only a very small number of the most elite competitors make it to Olympic or professional squads. The vast majority of sportsmen and women in the USA cease participating in high-level sport when they leave college or university. Hemery also comments that in a sport like athletics, where the trend is to reach a peak around the mid-twenties to mid-thirties, many of the better athletes have stopped competing years before they reach anywhere near their potential.

In the UK, most of the funding and support for elite sport has traditionally come from the voluntary and amateur sectors. Prior to the existence of the National Lottery, the funding of most programmes of sports excellence was based on donations, sponsorship and fund-raising activities from within sports organisations. Agencies such as the Sports Aid Foundation worked tirelessly to raise sufficient funds to provide a small number of elite performers with grants to help cover the cost of training and travel.

Since the introduction of the National Lottery in 1997, elite sports programmes have received a much-needed injection of cash, and this has enabled the building of a network of sports institutes and a broadening of the programmes they are able to offer. However, it must be remembered that this funding is reliant on the UK population continuing to buy tickets for the twice-weekly national lottery draws.

REVIEW QUESTIONS

1   Name and describe the four stages of the sports performance pyramid. .
2   Describe how sports can act as a shop window for a nation or culture
3   Why are governments keen to support elite sports programmes?
4   Describe the elite sports-excellence model.
5   Describe the optimum performance model of sports excellence.
6   What are the advantages of the elite sports model?
7   What are the limitations of the optimum performance model?
8   How does the USA nurture its potential elite athletes?
9   How does the US system compare with the excellence system in the UK?
10 Discuss why sports agencies in the UK may have been reluctant to adopt global systems of sports excellence.

9

Texts referred to in this chapter

Cashmore, E. (2005) *Making Sense of Sports*, 4th edn, London and New York: Routledge.

Hemery, D. (1991) *Sporting Excellence: What Makes a Champion*, London: CollinsWillow.

10

sporting excellence: the concept

chapter two

SPORTING EXCELLENCE
An historical overview

In earlier times

The approach to sport valued by the ancient Greeks was that winning was everything. Being awarded the title, *Arête* (excellence) was the highest attainment in Greek society. The ancient Greeks went to great lengths in their preparations and provided the prototype forms of training for sport which are still practised by many sports performers today. Cashmore (2005) suggests that the very concept of athletic preparation was, and is, a fundamental element in achieving sports excellence.

Recognition that 'excellence does not spring spontaneously but is the product of periods of heavy labour and disciplined regimes' prompted the Greeks to provide specialised facilities for training and preparation. These facilities, which began to appear around the sixth century BC, included gymnasia and other purpose-built training facilities along with staff and equipment which were aimed at preparing young men for competitive sport.

The quest for sporting excellence in the UK really began with the development of professional sports during the seventeenth and early eighteenth centuries. These sports made extensive use of footmen, servants and other 'paid retainers' by the gentlemen of the upper classes, with these men representing their 'patrons' in foot races, prize fights and in horse racing.

The practice was also common in cricket, with many estate workers being employed purely because of their sporting ability – often their bowling prowess – so that they could represent the master's team.

The motivation for all of these activities was wagering, which took place at almost any and every opportunity in both sport and in life generally. The quest for sporting champions was also fuelled by the desire of upper-class patrons to increase their standing amongst their peers in addition to a chance of winning what were often quite considerable prize funds and wagers.

British public schools

By the late nineteenth century, there had been a social shift in the terms of how sporting excellence was perceived. The best performers were by then almost exclusively drawn from the middle and upper classes and were all products of the expanding public-schools system. Sport in these schools was a product of the 'games ethic' (see Plate 2.1), which was itself born out of the principles of muscular Christianity.

Very quickly, however, sporting prowess – achieved either as an individual or as a member of a team – became highly valued in an educational system which had not yet become weighed down with the distractions of exam results and league tables. Sporting success also became an important marketing tool in attracting scholars and their fee-paying parents to a particular school.

PLATE 2.1 The Eton wall game: the 'games ethic' in action.

Photo: Eton College.

In order to help build their collective sporting reputation, these schools began to take such activities very seriously indeed, giving pupils ample time to practise and compete in their chosen sports. Increasingly, extravagant facilities were built, including extensive playing fields, sports pavilions, practice grounds, gymnasia and swimming pools in order to assist in this aim.

It became increasingly common for public and other independent schools to employ 'professionals' whose role was to coach and provide pupils with skilful opponents. In games such as cricket and racquet sports, these professionals became very commonplace and, in reality, represented the first attempt at systematic sports preparation.

The Headmaster of Uppingham School employed a cricket professional in 1870: 'not to have one has become equivalent to losing rank as a school' (Smith 1974: 47).

Into the 'melting pot' . . .

The two leading universities of Cambridge and Oxford readily took up this enthusiasm for sport, and their rivalry developed into a series of sporting events, which, by the end of the nineteenth century, had come to represent the very pinnacle of elite sport in England.

For the remainder of the nineteenth and much of the first part of the twentieth centuries, Oxbridge sportsmen figured largely in the framing of 'national' rules, the formation of national associations and in the leading domestic and international amateur sports teams.

Most of the current governing bodies of sport were formed during the last half of the nineteenth century, with former public schoolboys from Oxford and Cambridge being involved in nearly all of them. The University Boat Race, together with its corresponding fixtures in athletics, cricket, football and rugby became major features of the British sporting calendar.

Students who competed in these annual 'varsity' matches in their chosen sport were awarded a 'blue' and became part of the first elite band of sportsmen in the UK. Their contemporary and subsequent influence on the development of sport was huge, not only because of their dominance of early domestic and international teams but also because of their involvement in the diffusion of British sporting values both at home and abroad.

13

Diffusion

As British sport and sporting values spread around the world via the British Empire and its trading connections, new countries took up these same activities with a zeal that very quickly spawned international fixtures (see Figure 2.1).

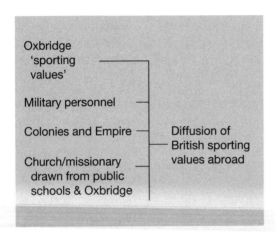

FIGURE 2.1
The diffusion of sport throughout the British Empire paved the way for 'global' sport.

It was equally quickly recognised by many of Britain's colonial outposts that sport offered them an early opportunity to test themselves against other nations – particularly the 'mother country'.

The term 'Test Match' was coined in the late nineteenth century by Australian cricketers as they prepared for a series of matches against England. They clearly saw victory at cricket as a reflection of both their independence and their sporting progress.

The benefits that came to be associated with international sporting success meant that teams and athletes began to look more closely (albeit often reluctantly) at specialised methods of training and preparation which had hitherto been regarded as cheating.

The rebirth of 'Olympism'

Another early major focus for the development of excellence in sport was the inauguration of the modern Olympic Games in 1896. Although Baron de Coubertin's ideal was one of a global competition allowing fellow athletes to test themselves against others in a spirit of friendship, both individual athletes and their respective countries soon became aware of the kudos that a good performance could bring. From the time of first modern games in Athens through to those of the present day, the unofficial medal table gradually became – and remains – a major focus.

It is interesting to note that the US team 'won' the first games in 1896, by which time they had already begun the process of systematic training at their universities. This was the forerunner of the 'athletic scholarship' which has remained the cornerstone of sports excellence in the USA until the present day (see Chapter 7).

However, the prevailing philosophy of those times was one of Corinthian purity, which required athletic performances to arise out of natural (God-given) talent rather than be the product of practice or inordinate amounts of time spent on the training ground – a practice which was generally frowned upon. It was this approach that so infuriated Harold Abrahams, whose story forms a central part of the film *Chariots of Fire*. Abrahams employed a professional coach, Sam Mussabini, in order to enhance his pursuit of an Olympic medal. This practice met with strong disapproval at the time, but, because it often brought success, was very soon taken up by a number of other athletes.

Amateur sport, which was often defined as participation 'purely for the enjoyment of sport', was in fact purely and simply a means by which members of the lower social orders were excluded from the 'sporting preserves' of the gentlemen of the increasingly influential middle classes (see Figure 2.2). Hutchinson (1996) argues that amateurism was written into the legislative body of British sport by the moneyed classes in order to keep out the lower orders. Amateurism was, from

Excellence
drawn from public
schools & Oxbridge

Bar to access
for those deemed
socially unacceptable

FIGURE 2.2
The nineteenth-century
sports-participation pyramid.

its earliest days in the middle of the nineteenth century, nothing more than a crude device of social exclusion, but by the early decades of the twentieth century, the rest of the world was gaining ground, and the exclusive position Britain had held at the head of world sport was under threat.

Hutchinson also notes that, 'a nation of [then] 45 million could not expect to get a thousand million playing its games – 400 million in the British empire, as well as the rest of Europe, Asia and the Americas – and continue to beat them' (1996: 83).

By the time the Olympic Games was held in London in 1908, sporting commentators felt obliged to remind their readers that the British team would have to work hard to beat the rest of the world. The team did not let them down, but the games of 1908 were to be the last great show of British sporting supremacy.

Great Britain (England, Ireland, Scotland and Wales) won 146 medals, fifty-six of them gold, whilst the second nation, the USA, was way behind with forty-seven medals in total, of which twenty-three were gold.

It is also interesting to note that the 1908 games were the first at which gold medals were awarded to the winners of Olympic finals. Previously, the winners' medals had been silver.

Changing times

A new world order was developing in international sport. The Americans and the nations of the southern hemisphere, as well as other European nations, were never really happy with the creed of 'British amateurism'. It became increasingly common for public and other independent schools to employ 'professionals' whose role was to coach and provide pupils with skilful opponents. This had been born out of the rigid class system nurtured on the playing fields of English public schools, which, whilst it had its equivalents in other cultures, was rather more entrenched there, albeit with a small number of exceptions.

The 1908 Olympics also witnessed a form of commercial patronage now more commonly referred to as 'sponsorship', namely commercial assistance to aid preparation. Dobbs (1973) notes that the French cycle team were supplied with free cycles, free facilities and training expenses by British cycle firms in return for the publicity gained by the team's use of British cycles.

By 1912, Cambridge Blue Philip Noel Baker was forced to lament that the typical American athlete was one who, 'Specialises in only one or two events. Before any

16

race of great importance he devotes most of his energies and his time to his training; he has a coach – often a professional – who likewise devotes his whole time and energies to his coaching' (Hutchinson 1996: 155).

Nationalism and sporting success

The First World War brought a temporary halt to the development of sport, with all major competitions being suspended. Much was made at that time of the link between those personal characteristics which were developed through sport and those needed in times of conflict. Sportsmen of all abilities were encouraged to sign up to fight for their respective countries.

The Germany that emerged from the conflict, a defeated Germany, very quickly turned to a new political ideology and a new leader, whose ideas on sport were to have a major impact on global sport and leave many legacies.

When the National Socialist Movement came to power in Germany in 1933, it brought with it a number of revolutionary strategies with regard to sport. There appeared to be two key motives behind these strategies:

1   to ensure that all Germans would be physically fit and prepared to defend their country;
2   to create elite athletes who would raise Germany's profile internationally as well as having a positive effect on morale at home.

All coaches working in sport received some form of financial reward in the new Germany, but all were required to be working towards some form of certified qualification.

Naul and Hardman (2002) suggest that throughout the 1930s an increasing amount of research was carried out using anthropological measurement, biomechanics and physiological research into the improvement of performance and blood doping.

In a show of reconciliation (Germany had originally been awarded the games of 1916 which of course never took place) the International Olympic Committee (IOC) awarded both the winter and summer Olympic Games of 1936 to Germany, little knowing that this was playing straight into the hands of the new leader of Germany, Adolf Hitler (see Plate 2.2).

PLATE 2.2 Hitler planned to use the Olympic Games as a showcase for German supremacy.

Photo: IOC/Olympic Museums collections © IOC.

BOX 2.1 NATIONS ENTERING THE OLYMPIADS OF 1936

Summer: Afghanistan, Argentina, Australia, Austria, Bermuda, Belgium, Brazil, Bolivia, Bulgaria, Canada, Chile, China, Colombia, Costa Rica, Czechoslovakia, Denmark, Egypt, Estonia, Finland, France, Germany, Greece, Haiti, Hungary, Iceland, India, Italy, Japan, Malta, Mexico, Monaco, Latvia, Liechtenstein, Luxembourg, The Netherlands, New Zealand, Norway, Peru (withdrew during the games), Poland, Philippines, Portugal, Romania, South Africa, Spain, Sweden, Switzerland, Turkey, United Kingdom, United States of America, Uruguay and Yugoslavia.

Winter: Austria, Canada, Czechoslovakia, Belgium, Denmark, Estonia, Finland, France, Germany, Hungary, Italy, Latvia, The Netherlands, Norway, Poland, Romania, Sweden, Spain, Switzerland, United Kingdom, and United States of America.

TABLE 2.1 Leading medal-winning countries, 1936

Summary

Summer	G	S	B	Total
Germany	33	26	30	89
USA	24	20	12	56
Hungary	10	1	5	16
Italy	8	9	5	22
Finland	7	6	6	19
France	7	6	6	19
Sweden	6	5	9	30
Netherlands	6	4	7	17
Japan	5	4	7	15
Great Britain	4	7	3	14

Winter	G	S	B	Total
Norway	7	5	3	15
Sweden	2	2	3	7
Germany	3	3	0	6
Finland	1	2	3	6
Austria	1	1	2	4
USA	1	0	3	4
Switzerland	1	2	0	3
Great Britain	1	1	1	3
Canada	0	1	0	1
France	0	0	1	1

In *Mein Kampf* (1925), Hitler stated that the purpose of the Nazi-ruled physical-education system would be to ensure that a German boy should be as strong and stainless as steel, as durable as leather and as quick as a whippet. In order to help develop this 'ideal German', Hitler ensured that every school offered at least five hours of physical education a week for all pupils. Hitler's propaganda minister Josef Goebbels realised that the Olympic Games would provide a splendid opportunity to demonstrate German vision and organisational expertise.

It is interesting (and ironic) to note that the most controversial issue surrounding the winter games held at the then recently merged Garmisch-Partenkirchen was the fact that Great Britain won the Olympic Ice Hockey medal with a team much boosted by the inclusion of Canadian professionals. Their 'need to win' was so great that they ignored controversial issues centred on amateurism and nationality.

Facilities for both the summer and winter games of 1936 were exceptional and, in the opinion of many, were regarded as the best ever at that time. The summer games were based around the Deutsches Stadium, which seated 110,000 spectators, and the open-air swimming complex accommodated 18,000 spectators.

Athletes were housed in Olympic villages; the one for the summer games consisted of over 100 buildings, including a staggering thirty-eight separate dining rooms. However, female athletes were not allowed into the Olympic village and were housed separately at a nearby physical-training college. All athletes at the summer games also had access to a 400-metre track and an artificial lake for both swimming and rowing events.

Nazi Germany gained that country's highest-ever medal tally at these games, with a total of eighty-nine medals, of which thirty-three were gold. One of the key successes of the Nazi sports programme was the rise in women's sport, and, at the 1936 Olympics, Germany's women were at the top of the rankings.

The Soviet bloc

Following the Second World War, another force in international sport emerged, one whose approach to the attainment of excellence would shape programmes and attitudes around the world for many decades to come. The post-war alignment of states in eastern Europe created the eastern or Soviet bloc, which was dominated by the former Soviet Union (USSR). Although the USSR has since been consigned to the history books following the disintegration of the Communist system in the early 1990s, this culture also merits particular attention because of the phenomenal sporting success it achieved in such a short time.

In countries such as the USSR and the German Democratic Republic (GDR), sport was completely state-controlled. Every aspect of the preparation for sports was carefully planned and controlled, with success in international sport (the so-called 'sporting shop window') being the objective. The international sporting stage provided the ideal opportunity for the eastern bloc countries, both individually and collectively, to succeed and, in doing so, to show off the sporting products of its political system to the rest of the world.

Riordan (1981) states that the philosophy was, 'Every win for the soviet union was a win for the Communist system and undisputable proof that this system was superior to the capitalist system of the west.' There was also a government push to develop talent in a range of minor sports. What mattered for the Soviet system was winning medals. Edelman (1993) comments that a medal in the luge was as valued as a medal in basketball, and the Soviet aim was simply to win more medals than any other country. Sports that had a number of categories and, therefore, many chances for medals, such as athletics, swimming and weightlifting were particularly targeted.

Sport played a very important role in all the eastern bloc countries. Success was achieved as the result of a carefully structured system which included the fitness-testing of the entire population and which subsequently saw to it that those individuals identified has having talent were sent to centrally funded sports schools and training centres and, ultimately, on to national sports academies.

A system of Olympic style tournaments (Spartakiads) was at the centre of this process of sports-excellence production. Edelman describes the highly organised pyramidal structure of the Soviet sports system as having local, regional and republican competitions leading to a quadrennial sports festival. The national Spartakiad would always take place one year before the Olympics and was used as the final selection for the Olympic team.

Although much of the success of the eastern bloc countries has been attributed to the widespread use of drugs, this alone would not account for the level and rate of success. Performers also had the best coaches, facilities and support that was available, and centres such as the Neubrandenburg Institute in East Germany have since become the blueprint on which many present-day sports institutes all around the world are based.

Also of significant importance is the fact that sport in these eastern European societies reflected the egalitarian ideology of a system that fostered the belief that everyone was equal in status. Although, as history has shown, this theory did not always transpose well into everyday life, it did at least mean that in terms of sporting opportunity, everybody had a chance to exhibit their potential and, thus, had an equal chance of achieving success. If an individual was identified as possessing sporting talent, he or she would be selected for further specialised training and testing, irrespective of racial or social background. This ensured that the state had the widest possible base from which to select its national teams and sporting individuals.

The East German legacy

The reunification of Germany in October 1990 saw the dawn of a new era for German high-performance sport. Naul and Hardman (2002) acknowledge that two very different systems of sports science needed to be brought together, whereby the sport and science institutions of the former GDR had to be adapted in order to conform to the more open and accountable structure of the Federal Democratic Republic (FDR). All the former East German institutes and centres of physical culture, such as those at Leipzig and Berlin, became satellite centres of the new German Sport Institute Network.

The process of integrating sports-science support between the two formerly independent countries has not moved quite so smoothly. The peeling back of the Iron Curtain was accompanied by revelations of large-scale doping programmes and other dubious scientific practices. There was much public and official discussion, and all former GDR scientists who were to be employed in the scientific institutes of the newly unified Germany were required to submit to a test of their technical and political integrity. Many others, who had identified too strongly with the political system of the former GDR, left Germany and made their services available to high-performance sports centres elsewhere in the world. Many were employed in the Australian Institute Network. In response to the widespread allegations of drug-taking in the GDR, the German Government set up a review, and, from this, the *Reiter Commission Report* led to the introduction of comprehensive testing for all German sports performers during training and competition. Two publicly funded doping-control laboratories were also set up.

The rest of the world follows

With the increased globalisation of sport during the latter part of the twentieth century, combined with the ever-expanding television coverage and commercial potential for sport, many countries – both advanced and emergent – began studying and adapting the former eastern bloc systems of developing sports excellence to suit their own needs.

Some nations – such as the UK and the USA – retained their own more traditional approaches to excellence in sport or developed their own systems. In the UK, the Central Council of Physical Recreation (CCPR) had established national physical-training centres in order to aid the preparation of national teams. The first, Bisham Abbey, was opened in 1946, but it took until 1973 for there to be seven other such centres (renamed as national sports centres) around the country. More information on the UK national sports centres can be found in Chapter 3.

First there was France . . .

France was the first European nation to adopt a more centralised approach to sports excellence following a poor display at the 1960 Rome Olympics. That country's government responded by taking direct control of elite sport and set about developing programmes for sporting excellence that reflected the nation's need for international sporting success. The French National Institute of Sport and Physical Education (INSEP) was created in 1976 in order to provide a training and preparation base for the country's elite athletes. Further information on the role and success of INSEP can be found in Chapter 6.

And Australia too . . .

In the late 1970s, the Australian government decided that it too could play a legitimate role in actively assisting the development of its country's sporting talent. The result was, quite literally, the building of Australian Institute of Sport (AIS) in Canberra, which, after initial successes, was expanded to include a system of satellite institutes across Australia's states and territories.

Most of the funding for elite sports programmes in Australia comes from the government, with the declared aim of helping the development of sporting champions and, thus, enhancing national prestige. In most instances, 'business partners' in the form of the country's leading banks and business houses are welcome to assist in the financing of such ventures. More information on the background to the Australian sports system can be found in Chapter 5.

And then . . .

By the 1980s, China was also awakening to the lure of international sport. All Chinese schoolchildren were screened using national standard physical-fitness tests, and a network of sports schools was set up to accommodate talented youngsters. In these schools, the very best young athletes were trained and housed at key sport schools. Knutton et al. (1990) report on the success of the so-called 'three levels of training'. By the end of the 1980s, China had built fourteen physical-culture institutes around the country, catering for some 20,000 elite athletes.

Emergent and developing countries have also been developing elite sports programmes. Indeed, India began to develop its national institute of sports in

23

1961. Based in a former royal palace, the institute provides training facilities, accommodation and sport-science support for students, national players and coaches.

Korea built its national sports-science institute during the preparations for its role as host for the 1988 Olympics, a move which has recently been repeated by the Greek government in preparation for their hosting of the Athens Games in 2004.

It is important for the home nation to do well at the games, and governments are willing to fund elite sport in return for success both in the stadium and beyond. Hosting global games such as an Olympics also means that athletes from the host country will have access to world-class facilities before and after the games. In Sydney, the warm-up track used by the Olympic athletes has now become part of a centre of excellence for Australian athletes.

REVIEW QUESTIONS

1   Is sports excellence a modern concept?
2   What role did the English public schools play in nurturing sporting talent in the nineteenth century?
3   Why did the UK's prominence in sport decline during the twentieth century?
4   How and why were games originating in the UK spread across the globe?
5   What factors led to Germany's interest in elite sport during the 1930s?
6   What factors led to East Germany's interest in elite sport during the 1960s?
7   Describe the systematic system of sports excellence developed in the GDR.
8   What elements of the GDR system are evident in modern elite sports programmes around the globe?
9   How do the French and Australian systems of sports excellence compare with those in the UK?
10 What problems do emergent and developing cultures face in creating systems of sports excellence?

Texts referred to in this chapter

Cashmore, E. (2005) *Making Sense of Sports*, 4th edn, London and New York: Routledge.

Dobbs, B. (1973) *Edwardians at Play: Sport, 1890–1914*, London: Pelham Books.

Edelman, R. (1993) *Serious Fun: A History of Spectator Sport in the USSR*, Oxford: Oxford University Press.

Hutchinson, R. (1996) *Empire Games*, London: Mainstream Publishing.

Holt, R. (1996) 'Patriotism', in D. Levinson and K. Christensen (eds) *Encyclopaedia of World Sport*, Oxford: Oxford University Press.

Knutton, H., Ma, Q. and Wu, Z. (1990) *Sport in China*, Champaign, Ill.: Human Kinetics.

Naul, R. and Hardman, K. (2002) *Sport and Physical Education in Germany*, London and New York: Routledge.

Riordan, J. (ed.) (1981) *Sport Under Communism*, 2nd edn, London: Hurst.

Smith, W. D. (1974) *Stretching Their bodies: The History of PE*, Newton Abbot: David & Charles.

chapter three

THE LONG WINDING PATH
Sports excellence in the UK, 1950–90

'In the post-war Summer Olympics Great Britain has never finished higher than seventh in the unofficial medal table.'

Polley (1988: 45)

Traditionally, the search for talent in the UK has been rather a 'hit or miss' affair. The ethical division between amateurism and professionalism that has dominated sport during the past two centuries has also seen attempts to rationalise the search for talent treated with much suspicion and beset with difficulty. This is due to a traditionally 'recreational' approach to sport and the commonly held belief that sport is (or should be) a recreation rather than a career or an occupation. There is also a view in the UK that the early identification and 'forcing' of talent is undesirable on the basis that young people should experience as wide a spectrum of sport as possible without early specialisation.

Polley (1988) suggests that the debate about sports excellence in the UK was set in motion in the mid-twentieth century as a result of a growing popular feeling of national decline in international sport brought about by the continuing break-up of the Commonwealth, the Suez Crisis and the developing Cold War.

Coghlan (1990) put forward the view that in the 1960s, coverage of national and international sport events increased dramatically in both quality and quantity alongside the advance of media technology. This helped to build a growing awareness amongst the general public that Britain's international sporting status was, perhaps, less than it might be.

The renegotiation of Britain's role in world politics was played out alongside a growing acceptance that British sporting superiority could no longer be assumed. This feeling was particularly enhanced by the famous defeats of the England football team by Hungary in 1953 and 1954 and the solitary gold medal won by Britain at the 1952 Olympic Games in Helsinki, won by a horse named Foxhunter.

With television quickly entering almost every UK home, sports programmes and events were watched by an increasing number of people, and, consequently, the debate about how sport should be organised gained momentum. Contemporary commentators laid the blame at the feet of the government, claiming that a lack of both interest and state funding had led to this decline. Indeed, both the Albemarle Committee of 1960 and the *Wolfenden Report* of the same year argued strongly for additional investment in facilities for sport and for investment in coaching. Both reports suggested that this should be in the form of grant-aid given by central government to the national sport agencies.

BOX 3.1 THE ALBEMARLE AND WOLFENDEN COMMITTEE

The Albemarle Committee was established in 1958 to review the Youth Service, whose stated dual responsibility was social and physical training with the aim of bringing 'young people into a normal relationship with their fellows and to develop bodily fitness' (Albemarle Report 1960: 8).

The Wolfenden Committee was formed by the CCPR in the late 1950s in response to a feeling within the CCPR that the government was not adequately supporting youth sport. Houlihan and White (2002) report that the Committee was given very broad terms of reference:
(a) to examine the factors affecting the development of games, sport and outdoor activities in the UK; and (b) to make recommendations to the CCPR as to any practical measure which should be taken by statutory or voluntary bodies.

A group of physical educationalists at the University of Birmingham went further, investigating this issue in their pamphlet, *Britain in the World of Sport* (1956). This bemoaned the inadequacy of support given to the country's elite athletes in preparing for international competition. There are remarkable similarities here to the way in which the British press laid the blame for the decline of British sport in the early 1990s squarely at the door of the then Prime Minister John Major, whose own failings were measured alongside those of the ineffective managers of English cricket and football teams.

The CCPR and onwards

The first real attempt to develop an organised approach to sports excellence in the UK occurred shortly after the Second World War, with the CCPR being given the initial responsibility for establishing national physical recreation centres. These now exist at:

- Bisham Abbey (1947)
- Lilleshall Hall (1951)
- Plas-y-Brenin (1954)
- Crystal Palace (1964)
- Cowes National Sailing Centre (1968)
- The National Sports Centre for Wales (1972)
- Holme Pierrepont Water Sports Centre (1973).

In Scotland, an outdoor sports centre was established at Glenmore Lodge in 1948. Many of these sports centres have now been remodelled as part of the current United Kingdom Sports Institute (see Chapter 9).

Bisham Abbey was the first centre, established in 1947, and is still used by many national teams as they prepare for international fixtures. The twelfth-century stately home was sold to the CCPR by Phyllis Vansittart-Neale in memory of two nephews killed during the Second World War. It is currently the training centre for England football and hockey teams and is the headquarters of the national tennis, judo, hockey and weightlifting associations.

In 1949, the CCPR were seeking a second national recreation centre for the north of England to complement the provision made by Bisham Abbey for the population in the southern counties. Mr Basil McNay of the CCPR identified Lilleshall Hall as a suitable site, and, although not strictly in the north but in Shropshire, it became a national sports centre in 1951, thanks mainly to fund-raising efforts by the South African government in appreciation of the UK's assistance during the Second World War. With over 30 acres of playing fields and artificial pitches, as well as indoor facilities and accommodation for 180 athletes, the centre can provide a supportive environment for an extensive range of sports. It currently houses the headquarters of the British Amateur Gymnastics Association (BAGA) and the National Sports Rehabilitation Centre.

In 1984, Lilleshall Hall was the site of a major attempt to promote excellence in football coaching and education. The Football Association (FA) National School of Excellence was established at the centre in order to provide teenage boys with the opportunity to develop their footballing skills whilst still continuing their normal education at nearby Idsall School in Shifnal, Shropshire. This was a revolutionary new approach to sports excellence in the UK. The boys were able to prepare for a professional playing career, and the venture also helped to lay the foundations for the development of a specialist sports college programme in UK state schools. Its very success brought about the closure of the school in 1999. Its example had led to the establishment of football academies by the leading clubs, which fulfilled the same role but provided a more direct link to a professional playing career for their students.

The Lawn Tennis Association (LTA) established a similar scheme with the National Tennis School at Bisham Abbey in 1982. With financial support from Rover, this centre offered a very small number of elite young tennis players a residential training base. Whilst this had some initial success, the idea of removing children from their home environment to live at a national centre was soon considered unwise. The LTA has since replaced its national centre with regional tennis centres around the country. These fulfil the same function as Bisham Abbey without the necessity for young people to live away from home.

Perhaps more successful in fulfilling its role has been the National Watersports Centre at Holme Pierrepont, Nottingham. This centre, built from reclaimed gravel pits in 1972, developed the first still-water multilane 2,000-metre rowing course in Britain and has become a centre of excellence for rowing in addition to a number of other sports. In 1986, a purpose-built white-water canoeing course was added.

The main limitation of these centres is, once again, related to the autonomy of the British sports governing bodies and the continual restructuring of the Sports Council in its various guises.

The growth of the Sports Council

Initially coordinated by the CCPR, this body was forced to transfer all its assets, including the national sports centres, to the then newly formed Sports Council in 1972. Due to a lack of revenue and worries over funding, the Sports Council then moved towards granting these centres self-management status, which ultimately led to the loss of the Cowes National Sailing Centre and forced the remaining centres to change their focus towards revenue-generating activities such as conferences and school visits.

Nearly there: centres of excellence

A government White Paper, *Sport and Recreation* (HMSO 1975) reviewed the provision for sports excellence in the UK and concluded that there needed to be a more imaginative approach to utilising the nation's athletics resources at every level of sport in society. This was the first White Paper ever published on sport and recreation. Coghlan (1990) reports that as a statement of policy it was warmly welcomed, and amongst its many conclusions was one specifically relating to gifted sportsmen and women. A special study of how talented sportsmen and women could be further assisted was promised. For the first time in any official sense, the need for centres of excellence was identified. It was suggested that universities and colleges might well play an important role in fulfilling this need.

Coghlan also suggests that although the proposed development of the Sports Aid Foundation was not mentioned specifically, the many references to the need to assist elite athletes more imaginatively and generously gave a clear early indication of the government's interest in setting up the foundation to help in this area of concern.

By the beginning of the 1980s, it was acknowledged that the funding of programmes of excellence was becoming a major issue in the UK. The Howell Report, a committee of enquiry into sports sponsorship set up by the CCPR, reported in December 1983 that, 'the pursuit of sporting excellence now makes demands on athletes almost beyond the call of duty. Sponsorship can offer some of these sport stars a chance to secure their financial future . . . such opportunities lay enormous responsibilities upon governing bodies' (Sports Council 1983).

The response from the sporting bodies was, as always, a compromise. Rules were altered to allow small number of elite athletes to set up trust funds in order to enable them to receive both commercial sponsorship in addition to (then) rather more dubious prize and appearance money.

Two foundations would play an important part in the preparation of elite athletes through the 1980s and 1990s, and, again, in true tradition, both were largely run and organised by dedicated amateurs:

- The Sports Aid Foundation;
- The National Coaching Foundation.

The Sports Aid Foundation

Actually set up as a charitable organisation in 1975, the Sports Aid Foundation (now rebranded Sports Aid UK) had as its aim the provision of funds that would enable athletes to train and prepare for international competition. Coghlan (1990) notes that in the three years before the Seoul Olympics, the Sports Aid Foundation provided £1.19 million in funds to Britain's Olympic athletes. The organisation raised this money by attracting support and financial contributions from commerce, business and generous patrons.

The National Coaching Foundation

The other organisation, established in 1983, was the National Coaching Foundation (now also rebranded as 'Sports Coach UK'). Coghlan suggests that the need for some centralised coaching service to assist in the training of sports coaches at all levels had been identified in 1975. However, an initial attempt to set up a unit at Loughborough University failed, due to a lack of funding and a reluctance on the part of other universities to support the venture.

The introduction of regional sports councils in the early 1980s saw the development of a number of coaching courses and workshops across the regions, and these were so successful that there was a new call for some form of national initiative. The Sports Council took up the challenge. Drawing on the experience of sports systems developed in both East and West Germany, and in light of the then existing British situation, it was decided that a network system could best embrace all that was currently going on in sports-science research in universities and colleges. These higher-education centres would make up the coaching units, with Leeds Polytechnic hosting the national headquarters.

The Sport Council committed £50,000 for the first year's budget, and it was agreed that the new organisation would be called the National Coaching Foundation (NCF) and would be managed by an independent committee. The NCF has been extremely successful in developing a range of resources and aids for coaches as well as extending the knowledge of many thousands of coaches through its courses and workshops.

In a government policy document on sport, *The Government's Plan for Sport* (Department of Culture, Media and Sport 2000: 29, 31), the role of Sports Coach UK is seen as being central within the 'World Class' programme: 'The Government recognises that coaching is central to development of sport at every level.'

The government's proposals for coaching in the UK included establishing a coaching task force to undertake a review of coach education and consider the feasibility of creating 3,000 full-time coaches and the introduction of a licensing system for all sports coaches.

So, as sport in the UK approached the end of the second millennium, there were some systems in place, but there appeared to be a large number of bodies looking after the interests of a comparatively small number of elite performers, both in terms of financial support and the type of assistance required to compete globally in sport.

REVIEW QUESTIONS

1 How might traditional sporting views in the UK have constrained any moves towards policies of sports excellence?
2 Discuss the concepts of amateurism and professionalism in terms of elite sport.
3 Why was the UK government reluctant to support elite sport financially during the mid-twentieth century?
4 Why might UK sports agencies have been reluctant to receive state funding?
5 What was the initial role of the national physical recreation centres?
6 How has this role changed over the past thirty years?
7 What impact did the newly established Sports Council have on elite sport in the 1970s?
8 What role does Sports Coach UK have in the development of elite sport in the UK?
9 What factors led to the establishment of National Sports centres in the UK?
10 Can you identify how the UK has used comparative study in the setting up of its elite sports system?

Texts referred to in this chapter

Coghlan, J. F. (1990) *Sport and British Politics since 1960*, London: Falmer.
Department of Culture, Media and Sport (2000) *A Sporting Future for All: The Government's Plan for Sport*, London: DCMS.

HMSO (1975) 'Nearly There: Centres of Excellence', A Government White Paper – *Sport and Recreation*, London: HMSO.

Houlihan, B. and White, A. (2002) *The Politics of Sports Development*, London and New York: Routledge.

Polley, M. (1988) *Moving the Goal Posts*, London and New York: Routledge.

Sports Council (1983) *The Howell Report*, London: Sports Council.

chapter four

ATLANTA 1996
An Olympic failure too far

'It was July 23rd 1996 and hopes of a glorious summer of sporting success for Britain seemed to have been dashed. Our footballers had failed at Euro '96, our cricketers were being flayed by Pakistan and at the Atlanta Olympics the TV presenters' expectant smiles were beginning to crack along with the nation's patience.'

Bent et al. (2001)

Atlanta: the cold facts

The final medal total of one gold, eight silver, six bronze and thirty-sixth position on the medal table was Britain's worst Olympic result since the 1952 Helsinki Games – when the only gold medal was won by a horse!

Linford Christie, athletics captain and defending Olympic Champion, was disqualified in the 100-metres final and did not qualify for the 200-metres final. Former World 110-Metres Hurdles Champion Colin Jackson did not place, and Scots cyclist Graeme Obree, World-Record Holder in the men's individual pursuit, was knocked out in the first heat. All in all, it was a sorry performance and led many from both sport and the media to question the reasons for it.

'I have a message for [Prime Minister] John Major', said the Head of the British Olympic Association, Richard Palmer, 'we need more money'. Malcolm Arnold, Head Coach of the British Athletics Federation, who, in an interview with the *Daily Telegraph*, attacked the lack of government funding, echoed this view. He was of the opinion that if more money and resources were not immediately available, it could be 2004 or 2008 before Britain could again expect to do well in an Olympics.

Arnold went on to state that many of the athletes competing at the games of 1996 would simply return to their former careers after the games – thus highlighting the point that the need for greater funding had to be matched by the equally important matter of using it well: 'It is not a simple matter to produce champions of tomorrow and it often takes six, seven or eight years to maximise an athlete's potential, so delays in receiving additional funding merely prolongs the developmental process' (Arnold 1996).

There was also the small matter of the BBC *Panorama* programme shown three weeks before the games, which suggested that drug abuse was rife amongst the world's top athletes. This, claimed Arnold, had destroyed the British team's morale, which had been high until remarks were made in the media about the number of British athletes allegedly involved in drug abuse.

The *Daily Telegraph* also raised another key point: that hardly any fresh talent had emerged in 1996 to replace the luminaries who had brought home a suitcase full of medals from Barcelona in 1992 and who, in doing so, had created a false picture of the health of British athletics.

Britain's medal count at the Atlanta Games was the stuff of spoofs, but it did illustrate the British tendency to become mired in bureaucracy and circular arguments while the rest of the world races ahead. The same debates about amateur administrators and the lack of funding also crop up in tennis, cricket and rugby. The 'blazerocracy' that controls so much of British sport is in retreat but still fighting. A case of cocktails and cock-ups being inextricably linked (see Figure 4.1).

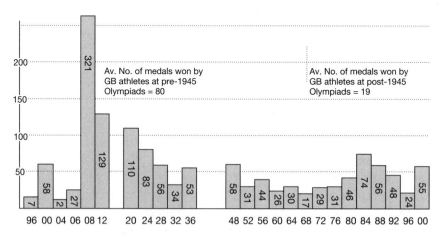

FIGURE 4.1 GB medal totals since the beginning of the modern Olympics.

atlanta 1996: an olympic failure too far

Shaking the tin: Team GB funding pre-1998

The British Olympic team is unique in receiving no official or state funding and relies on private donations and fund-raising. This is a major undertaking, with most money coming from one of two sources:

1   licensed merchandise – the BOA licenses certain manufacturers to produce and distribute products with Olympic and BOA logos in the UK;
2   The British Olympic Appeal: donations from individuals, organisations and companies are collected through a nationwide appeal. These donations do not confer any promotional or other rights.

Prior to the 1996 games, this included an appeal in the USA to raise 2 million dollars so that Great Britain could send a full team.

'Raising the game'

Prior to the games of 1996, the Prime Minister John Major, along with Sports Minister Ian Sproat, published a policy document entitled *Sport: Raising the Game* (HMSO 1995). This document, which set out the government's commitment to sport, also outlined the refocused role of the Sports Council. The main strategy was an increased emphasis on sport for school-aged children, and, more importantly, the development of support for the performance and excellence sectors. This again reflected the theory that by widening the participation base, there would be an eventual increase in the number of elite performers.

Raising the Game was, in fact, the first recognition by the authorities in the UK that success at elite levels of competition could no longer be achieved without systematic application of the highest standards of sports science and coaching to squads of full-time athletes.

Sports Minister Sproat stated in the 1995 document, *Sport for All – RIP*, that the Sports Council would 'withdraw from the promotion of mass participation and informal recreation'. This represented a clear shift of policy and put high performance at the centre of sports development in the UK. Houlihan and White (2002) report that the centrepiece of this policy statement was the commitment to establish an elite sports training centre in the form of a British Academy of Sport, modelled on the successful Australian Institute of Sport (AIS) at Canberra.

Underwritten by funds from the newly established National Lottery, the academy was intended to provide top-class training facilities, coupled with a concentration

37

FIGURE 4.2
The National Lottery has
been a major source of
funding for elite sport in
the UK.

of support services such as coaching, sports science and sports medicine. In addition, the Sports Council was to assist the national governing bodies of sport to develop talent-identification programmes (see Figure 4.2).

Houlihan and White conclude with the suggestion that it was John Major who finally put the myth of the inspired British amateur to rest and showed that even the British government had grown to understand that success in international sport matters – and costs! Unfortunately for John Major, this was to be one of his last acts as prime minister before New Labour swept to victory in the 1997 General Election.

New Prime Minister Tony Blair adopted most of the Conservative polices on sport, although he renamed both the department responsible for sport and the fledgling academy to give them both a degree of 'Labour ownership'. Under Blair, the Department of National Heritage became the Department of Culture, Media and Sport (DCMS) and the British Sports Academy became the United Kingdom Sports Institute (UKSI).

The government continued to recognise and support the view that the only means of Britain achieving success in the global sporting arena was through a systematic and professional approach. Blair himself stated, 'We need to learn the lessons of our competitor nations and have the most professional system for talent development and support of excellence. The most talented 14-year-olds will be identified and offered a place at one of the sports colleges which in turn will be linked to the UKSI network' (Blair 2000).

However, problems had begun to appear even before Major had left office. Most of the ideas for the new academy had been based on the successful AIS (see Chapter 5), and both Major and Sproat had visited the AIS in Australia's capital, returning convinced that this was the answer to the UK's sporting malaise. But they appeared to have missed a key point. The AIS only worked as a successful 'finishing school' for Australian athletes because there was a strong and well-organised network below it encouraging participation at grass-roots level and systematically developing skills and creaming off the best talent. Bent et al. (2001: 46) concluded that, 'Sproat and his advisors were dazzled by what they saw – and paid less attention to what they could not see. They failed to grasp the importance of the "people" part of the mix.'

The UK government's proposal was more about bricks and mortar: building a highly visible 'hot house' that would give the politicians a nice photo opportunity and clear proof of their commitment to the UK's sporting future. So, although Major's government appeared to have a clear vision of what they wanted to produce, they dawdled. The Australian federal government, which, in 1980, had come up with a similar vision, simply paid a company to build an institute and then 'cherry-picked' the best sporting brains from around the world to run it.

In typically British fashion, the UK government announced it was going to hold a competition, inviting consortia to bid for the right to build and then run the academy. The Sports Council also consulted both elite athletes and the national governing bodies of sport . . . but seemed to ignore what it was being told. The summary to the 1996 consultation document records that when questioned about their needs in terms of elite preparation, most athletes talked about full-time training, money for coaches and access to a network of sports centres no more than an hour's drive from their home – not a central academy!

Whilst the 1996 consultation was being carried out, the Sports Council was also going through one of its regular phases of restructuring. The organisation had already changed from being a single quango based in London to become four separate councils based in each of the home countries. It was subsequently felt that there should also be one body to oversee sport on a UK basis, and so UK Sport was created.

The brief for this new body was to identify sporting policies that should have a UK-wide application and apply them. Obviously, the proposed academy of sport fell within this remit, although, since lottery funding was controlled and distributed by the four 'home' sport councils, UK Sport was immediately placed in a difficult situation as it had to go begging to them for necessary funds. Since the academy was to be based in England, the other three councils were reluctant to commit funding. The UK was still a long way from introducing a well-structured system of support for its elite athletes, and it was to be the spring of 1999 before a new plan was unveiled (see Chapter 9).

1 To whom do you think the term 'blazerocracy' refers?
2 Why does the BOA continue to self-fund?
3 Although *Raising the Game* was only an advisory document, many of the ideas it suggested have now become practice. Identify them.
4 Sport is now within the portfolio of the government Department of Culture, Media and Sport – discuss.
5 Where did the idea for a British sports academy come from?
6 What was the proposed role for the British sports academy?
7 What were the weaknesses of the Conservative government's plan for a British sports academy?
8 How did the incoming Labour government of 1997 adapt these plans?
9 What were the conclusions to the 1996 Sports Council survey of elite UK athletes concerning training needs?
10 How did the restructuring of the sports councils in 1996 further inhibit the development of a coherent elite sports system for the UK?

Texts referred to in this chapter

Arnold, M. (1996) quoted in *Daily Telegraph*, 23 September.

Bent, I., McIlroy, R., Mousley, K. and Walsh, P. (2001) *Blowing the Whistle: Five Live Investigates the Dark Side of Sport*, London Books.

Houlihan, B. and White, A. (2002) *The Politics of Sports Development*, London: Routledge.

Sproat, I. (2000) *A Sporting Future for All*, London: Department of Culture, Media and Sport.

chapter five

AUSTRALIA: WHY ARE THEY WINNING?

'Sport was the first form of Australian foreign policy. Until the British got into some wars to which the Australians could send volunteers, it was the only way in which Australians could prove they were best.'

Horne (1970)

'If we do what we did for the last Games we will be nowhere, if we follow the best practice internationally we may just be competitive, but if we fill each day with initiative we will win medals.'

Robert de Castella, Director, AIS, 1995,
in Dale and Cameron (1994: 137)

The Australian Institute of Sport (AIS) has led the development of elite sport in Australia for more than two decades, and its success is widely acknowledged by the Australian public. It is now internationally highly regarded as a world best-practice model for the development of elite athletes. Many countries, including the UK, are now actively engaged in setting up similar programmes in a bid to emulate Australia's sporting success.

Sport is a central element in Australian culture, and winning at sport has been an important goal throughout much of the country's history, beginning with the famous first 'test' victory over England in 1882 and, more recently, with the success at the Sydney Olympic Games in 2000. Dunstan (1973: 1) summarises, 'Sport is the ultimate Australian super-religion, the one thing every Australian believes in passionately. Sport is wholesome. It can do no wrong. It builds stronger Australian men and women, and best of all; it spreads the fame of Australians overseas. It helps unify Australia as a nation.'

The AIS was born out of Australia's disappointing performance at the 1976 Olympics in Montreal where just one silver and four bronze medals were won.

The country's federal government conducted a review of its elite sports systems and the outcome was a decision that the country needed a centre of excellence that would organise the preparation of athletes for international competition. The role of the centre (and its subsequent network of specialist centres) in developing sports excellence can be judged by the following facts:

- At the 1992 Olympics in Barcelona, Australia won twenty-seven medals, including seven gold.
- At the games in Sydney in 2000, this tally had risen to fifty-eight medals, of which sixteen were gold.

See also Table 5.1 below.

TABLE 5.1 **Australian Olympic medals: 'pre' and 'post' AIS**

Summer Olympic Games

	G	S	B	T
1956: Melbourne	13	8	14	35
1960: Rome	8	8	6	22
1964: Tokyo	6	2	10	18
1968: Mexico	5	7	5	17
1972: Munich	8	7	2	17
1976: Montreal	0	1	4	5
1980: Moscow	2	2	5	9
1984: Los Angeles	4	8	12	24
1988: Seoul	3	6	5	14
1992: Barcelona	7	9	11	27
1996: Atlanta	9	9	23	41
2000: Sydney	16	25	17	58
2004: Athens	17	16	16	49

Building success

The key was the wider public displeasure about the poor performance of Australia's athletes, and this gave the Australian federal government a mandate to spend large amounts of public money on creating an elite sports system that would ensure success at future international sports events.

Mangan and Nauright (2000) suggest that the foundation of the AIS was the first major step in the construction of a 'gold medal factory' that would ensure Australia's return to glory. They also suggest that the creation of the AIS and the increased financial support of elite sport by the Australian state throughout the 1980s were tied to the recognition that Australian sport could no longer match the successes of Communist nations without adopting organisational strategies and a more professional and scientific approach to producing gold-medal-winning athletes.

The AIS was opened on 'Australia Day' 1981 on a 65 hectare site, just ten minutes from Canberra's city centre. The first intake of 150 athletes in eight sports (basketball, swimming, weightlifting, track and field, gymnastics, netball, soccer and tennis) was based in Canberra. The AIS now offers scholarships to almost 600 athletes each year in thirty-two separate programmes covering twenty-five sports and employs around seventy-five full time coaches across a range of sports.

Though most of the focus sports have been Olympic ones, there are now plans to expand the role of the AIS to accommodate a wider range of sports programmes which will be located in satellite institutes around Australia in places such as Adelaide, Perth, Brisbane, Melbourne, Sydney, the Gold Coast and Mount Buller.

The AIS is the pre-eminent elite sports-training institution in Australia and provides athletes with world-class training facilities. This includes high-performance coaching, state-of-the-art equipment, top-class sports medicine and sports science, travel, accommodation for up to 350 on site and refunding of education expenses.

Seeking out the talent

One of the most successful sports-science experiments developed by the AIS was 'Sports Search', a talent-identification programme. The rising cost of preparing elite athletes (the 1998 AIS budget was £7 million) has meant that Australia has had to become more cost-conscious in targeting its potential talent. This is further exacerbated by the country's relatively small population of 19 million, compared with the 58 million in the UK.

In 1988, a small group of sports scientists based at the AIS undertook an analysis of all the rowers taking part at the Australian national championships. Rowing had been identified as a sport which was relatively weak at international level, would fit well into the AIS model and should bring Australia success. The scientists were interested in the differences between those who won and those who lost in the various categories. What they discovered was that the rowers who won the races tended to share similar physical characteristics. It was concluded that the ideal rower should:

■   be tall;
■   be longer in the legs than in the back;
■   have long forearms;
■   have narrower hips than average;
■   have a greater level of endurance.

From this information, a bank of fitness tests and a number of required anatomical measurements were compiled in order to help identify this particular body type. These requirements were then circulated to a considerable number of high schools to assist with the early identification of potential talent.

In addition, it was decided that it would pay to concentrate on female rowers since it was felt that it would be easier to win medals in female rather than male events. This was due to the fact that rowing had one of the lowest levels of female participation around the world.

Adair and Vamplew (1997) report that between 1994 and 1996 Australian schools were asked to participate in a much broader-based national sports 'talent search' scheme in which pupils were subjected to tests of speed, strength and flexibility in an attempt to pinpoint speed, anatomical and physiological characteristics. The tests were designed by sports scientists at the AIS to measure suitability for Olympic sports. Scientists looked at muscle structure and aerobic capacities and predicted the combinations most likely to produce future champions. Afterwards students criticised this as an elitist approach since only 2 per cent of those tested were invited to take part in the second phase of testing. These were sport-specific testing programmes run by the state and regional academies and institutes of sport.

Sports science and research

The AIS also provides administrative, sports-science and coaching services and funding assistance to state and territory institutes and academies of sport and national sporting organisations. It is also at the leading edge of sports science and research developments. The Sports Science and Sports Medicine Division is credited with revolutionary breakthroughs, such as the ice jacket used at the Atlanta Olympics, the 'super-roo' bike and the use of the Altitude House as an important facility in helping athletes prepare for competition. This division boasts some of the world's leading authorities in physiology, biomechanics, psychology, nutrition and sports medicine.

There is no better example of the cutting-edge work of the AIS in sports science than the development of a test for EPO (Erythropoietin) now endorsed by the IOC Medical Commission and approved by its executive. This singular achievement has put Australia and AIS sports science and sports medicine on the world stage.

Since 1998, the AIS has moved away from its original centralised model, and, although the centre at Canberra still functions as the hub of the organisation, the AIS now offers support through a network of coaches and support staff based in the institutes in each of Australia's states. This evolution from a centralised to a decentralised system fits more comfortably into the country's federal/state political administration. This change is also the result of the other key factor in Australia's success, namely, that they are continually looking to review and improve their systems of sports excellence. It was found that athletes preferred to stay and live in their own locality and that extended residence at an institute was not always welcome or beneficial in terms of personal well-being or improved performance.

State institutes are largely non-residential and provide a central location for management, coaches, support services and medical and sports-science units. Before her retirement, Cathy Freeman preferred to live at her own home in Melbourne but had all the elite athlete support she needed from the Victorian Institute of Sport (VIS, Figure 5.1), which is based in that city.

And after sport . . .

Another support service to scholarship holders is the ground-breaking Athlete Career and Education (ACE) programme. This was set up to enhance the personal

FIGURE 5.1
The VIS in Melbourne: a state centre of sports excellence.

development and performance of Australia's elite athletes through a number of career and education services. Throughout Australia, a national network of advisers provide athletes with guidance on education, career-planning, job searching and personal development to make sure they plan for life after sport.

The following key features have, therefore, contributed to Australia's continued success in global sport:

- a strong national love of sport;
- significant public-sector funding at both federal and state level;
- effective comparative study and the resultant adoption of a high-performance culture.

1   What was the role of the AIS when it was established in 1981?
2   What were the reasons that led to the formation of the AIS?
3   What role does the Australian government play in that country's elite sports system?
4   How has the AIS developed to give a nationwide programme of elite sport?
5   What support does the AIS offer elite Australian sportsmen and women?

Texts referred to in this chapter

Adair, D. and Vamplew, W. (1997) *Sport in Australian History*, Oxford: Oxford University Press.

Dale, R. and Cameron, C. (1994) *The Contenders*, London: Boxtree.

Dunstan, K. (1973) *Sports*, North Melbourne: Cassell Australia.

Horne, D. (1970) *The Next Australia*, Sydney: Angus & Robertson.

Mangan, J.A. and Nauright, J. (2000) *Sport in Australasian Society*, London: Frank Cass.

chapter six

VIVE LA FRANCE!

The Institut National du Sport et de l'Education Physique (INSEP) was created in 1976 in order to provide a training and preparation base for France's elite athletes. In a string of events similar to that outlined in the Australian model, France had suffered a series of disappointing results at summer Olympic Games. This led to public outcry and subsequent state intervention, which eventually led to a comparative study of systems of sports excellence around the world. This study produced a complete overhaul of the elite sports system in France. Just outside Paris, at Vincennes, a national academy of sport was built which would be the centre for the training of athletes, coaches and teachers. It would provide French sports squads with the best possible facilities and support and was closely based on the East German elite sports model.

The whole of French sport was also taken under government control, and a new department, the Ministère de la Jeunesse et des Sports (Ministry of Youth and Sport) was created. This ministry now has ultimate responsibility for the development of sport in France and decides which sports and athletes shall have access to INSEP facilities and expertise. It also dictates the levels of funding that are available for the development of elite sport.

The INSEP site covers 34 hectares and caters for twenty-six sports. Facilities include:

- two swimming pools;
- indoor athletics track;
- indoor cycling track;
- gymnasium;
- football and rugby pitches;
- tennis and basketball courts;
- boxing rings, judo and fencing areas.

There is accommodation for up to 550 athletes, and there is also a full academic programme that can offer training in sports science, sport medicine and sports administration to athletes, coaches and administrators.

Each athlete receives funding for both training and competition, and athletes coming to the end of their career continue to receive funding for two years after their decision to retire. Whilst residing at INSEP, athletes receive teaching in sports-related courses, and INSEP also trains professional sports managers and coaches in addition to being a key centre for the training of teachers of physical education.

There are currently around 3,500 French sportsmen and women classed as elite performers who are, therefore, eligible for state funding. Approximately 500 are actually resident at INSEP, including a number of athletes from France's former (mainly North African) colonies. There are other elite performers who attend INSEP on a non-residential basis, in addition to those who are attached to regional 'mini-INSEPs', a feature that is also found in the Australian system.

These smaller regional centres, known in France by the acronym 'CREPS' (Centre d'Education Populaire et de Sport), were traditionally used to train physical-education teachers but are being increasingly used to nurture potential elite athletes. Examples of such centres and their specialisms include:

- Font Romeu: high-altitude training and gymnastics;
- Monceau-les-Mines: gymnastics;
- Aix-en-Provence: weightlifting;
- Vitell: swimming;
- Chamonix: skiing and mountain sports;
- Beg-Rohu: sailing and water sports;
- Saumur: national horse-riding school.

TABLE 6.1 **A typical day at INSEP for a fifteen-year-old swimmer**

7.00 a.m.	Breakfast
8.00 a.m.	Swim training in pool
10.00 a.m.	Theoretical studies (sports performance based)
1.00 p.m.	Lunch
2.00 p.m.	Rest
3.00 p.m.	General education and personal tutorial
6.00 p.m.	Land-based training and medical treatment
8.00 p.m.	Social/relaxation
9.30 p.m.	Back in study room
10.00 p.m.	Lights out

The Font Romeu centre, at a height of 1,850 metres in the centre of the Pyrenees, offers all French national sports squads the opportunity to train at high altitude.

The French elite sports system is very much a top-down model, with a great deal of state control, which is implemented specifically through the Ministry of Youth and Sport.

After the Second World War, the French President Charles de Gaulle made a commitment to use sport as a means of recreating a sense of national pride amongst the French people (not essentially very different from De Coubertin's philosophy in creating the modern Olympic movement at the end of the nineteenth century).

There continues to be a clear commitment from the French government with support for elite sports centres and athletes, including those from former French colonies.

The fall before the rise

The key date in the story of French sports excellence was 1960, the year in which France failed to win any gold medals at the Rome Olympics. For a country with a rich heritage of sport, especially at international level, this failure created a dent in national spirit and prestige.

In rebuilding France after the Second World War, President de Gaulle had visualised sport as a vehicle of nation-building. His philosophy was that the State must take up the organisation and financing of sport.

De Gaulle's response to Olympic failure in 1960 was to release the state aid which was needed to improve the facilities for sport throughout France. His dream was that every village and town should have:

- a swimming pool;
- a sports hall;
- a stadium.

He also believed that a central system of sports administration should be set up to promote a national policy of sport.

A planned sports pyramid

INSEP now caters for 850 elite French athletes, with satellite centres around the country such as the altitude-training centre at Font Romeu and the FFA Football Academy at Clare Fontaine outside Paris. These athletes are provided with top-class facilities and coaches as well as assistance with education and careers. Mirroring the state control of sport in France, INSEP is officially an arm of the Ministry of Youth and Sport. The institute liaises with the various French sporting federations who nominate the athletes with the potential to compete at international level.

Although approximately 850 athletes might be based at INSEP at any one time, there are around 3,500 athletes identified annually as having potential. Those not actually at INSEP are either already competing at an international level or are younger athletes based at 'mini INSEPs' (CREPs).

All France's identified elite athletes receive centralised (government) funding to assist with their training and competition costs, and this funding continues for two years after they have retired from competition. Put simply, this means that athletes who are good enough will get the funding they need.

CREPs are regional centres of sports excellence and are aimed at students still at school and provide localised back-up for potential elite performers. Currently there are twenty-three CREPS at:

- De Paca
- Ajaccio
- Mâcon
- Toulouse
- Montpellier
- Des Pays de la Loire
- Reims
- Wattignies
- Strasbourg
- Ile de France
- Limousin
- Réunion
- Houlgate
- Dijon
- Franche-Compté
- Bordeaux
- Dinard
- Centre
- Nancy
- Vichy
- Voiron
- Poitou-Charentes
- Antilles et la Guyane

A large amount of sports funding in France comes from the public sector. All public companies are required to invest a small percentage of their profits into social programmes, including sports development. The day-to-day funding of

INSEP comes mainly from the sports federations, who, in turn, receive a large amount of their income from the public purse.

As mentioned above, INSEP provides education and career guidance for elite athletes, and many undertake academic courses in sports science and sports management so that at the end of their sporting careers they can stay within the world of sport and possibly put something back into the system. INSEP is also the national training centre for sports managers and coaches. The French sports federations have now made it compulsory that any coach working in sport must achieve a nationally accredited qualification through INSEP.

It would appear that in terms of Olympic medals, France's long-term investment in its sporting youth seems to be paying off. From the low watermark of 1960 (no gold medals at all and only five medals in total), there has been a steady

TABLE 6.2 **French Olympic medals: the fall and rise**

Summer Olympic Games

	G	S	B	T
1956	4	4	6	14
1960	0	2	3	5
1964	1	8	6	15
1968	7	3	5	15
1972	2	4	7	13
1976	2	3	4	9
1980	6	5	3	14
1984	5	7	16	28
1988	6	4	6	16
1992	8	5	16	29
1996	15	7	15	37
2000	13	14	11	38
2004	11	9	13	33

improvement to reach the current levels of relative success, which also included victory in the FIFA World Cup as host nation in 1998

REVIEW QUESTIONS

1   What was the role of INSEP when it was established in 1976?
2   What were the reasons that led to the formation of INSEP?
3   What part does the French government play in the elite sports system of France?
4   How has INSEP developed to provide a nationwide programme of elite sport?
5   What support does INSEP offer elite French sports men and women?

chapter seven

USA: NO. 1

The sporting dream

A distinctive feature of sport in the USA is the way in which sporting talent is nurtured through the high-school and college system. It is this system which will be the focus of this part of the chapter. Although unique to the USA, it is a system which is now being experimented with in a number of other cultures; indeed, the growth of sports colleges and university sports scholarships in the UK has, in some ways, been shaped by the success of the system across the Atlantic.

Bale (1994) has highlighted how the US system of youth sport, which is focused almost exclusively on the school and college system, is completely different from the club-based focus in most European countries. High-school and college sport in the USA is a mirror of its professional sports system, and most high schools possess lavish facilities for both players and spectators.

Another key feature is the support that school and college teams receive from their local communities. In many towns, school sport is almost a religion, with huge crowds attending both games and practices. Often this support includes a considerable financial input, which goes some way to explaining the high standards of performance and coaching.

Intercollegiate Athletics in the USA was born in 1852 with a series of rowing matches between Harvard and Yale universities, and, although these and other early activities were initially organised, funded and conducted by interested students, their popularity was such that, before long, university administrators took control of sport. Coaches were hired and sporting 'programmes' were built, and intercollegiate sport came to be regarded as a phenomenon that could increase the prestige of an institution and attract future students. The level and standard of play are unquestionably high, and the rivalry in the local school leagues is intense, with competitions at local, district and regional levels leading to state championships and, at college level, a national final.

The fundamental connection between sport in the high schools, colleges and the professional leagues is the unique system of athletic recruitment practised in the USA. This is the selection process whereby students move from high school by means of an athletic scholarship into college sport programmes and then, if good enough, enter professional sport by means of the annual 'draft' (see Figure 7.1). The chances of that are very slim indeed.

Although it is the dream of the majority of aspiring school and college athletes to reach the professional game, it must be noted that to do so means enduring a very elitist and competitive process. Bale (1994: 23) notes that: 'in American football only 4.2% of high school first team players progress to the draft stage of recruitment. In basketball the figure is only 2.2%.'

Excellence
Professional sport:
Entry via the 'draft' system
from college sport

College sport
programs
Athletic scholarships

High School ('varsity')
sport programs
Junior high school sport

'Kiddie', 'Pee-wee' and other
early sport programs
Early school age participants

FIGURE 7.1
Sports-participation pyramid, USA.

Be that as it may, high-school sport is, in the vast majority of cases the only way to the top in most major sports in the USA. There is, therefore, little alternative for those who wish to make it than to 'get noticed' and hope that several years of slavish adherence to the rules of the system will get them to their goal and, at the very least, a free college education.

High-school sport and the nurture of talent

High-school sport is the starting point for athletes wishing to make a career out of sport. Sport in schools did not really develop until after the American Civil War, when the early Puritan influence in the new country had begun to wane. The Puritan ideal of the 'work ethic' had been instrumental in degrading any physical activity that had 'play' or 'recreational' associations, but after the Civil War, a system based on the British public-school sports model began to develop and quickly became widely adopted.

Currently, schools affiliate to their own local (state) high-school athletic associations, which in turn belong to the National Federation of State High Schools. These organisations coordinate and regulate sport and other physical activities.

Interschool sport reaches its greatest intensity during Grades 11 and 12 (the final high-school years), when students represent their school in a number of sports. Although the bigger schools do have teams in a range of sports, most tend to specialise in American football or basketball. This often follows a geographical pattern, with city schools concentrating on basketball and those in smaller towns playing football. Those selected to play in high-school basketball and football teams have their timetables altered so that they can train for a number of hours on schooldays, and most games take place on a Friday night in order to attract a large community following.

Schools initially play in local conferences or leagues where rivalry is intense, and the team with the best results at the end of a round-robin tournament then progresses to district and subsequently state championships.

Coaches are members of the high-school faculty and are sometimes teachers. The regulations here vary from state to state, and, although some high schools do employ teams of specialist coaches for their major teams, in some areas it is required that all coaches must be qualified teachers and have a minimum (but often nominal) teaching allocation. Conversely, it is now a requirement in many areas that teachers who intend to coach high-school sport must hold a recognised coaching qualification.

Teams have large budgets in order to fund the best possible equipment and preparation. This funding comes from gate money at home games and fund-raising activities by the school's 'booster club'. Booster clubs are another unique feature of school sport in the USA and usually involve local businessmen, former players and pupils. These clubs raise large amounts of money in order to help support 'their school' team.

College scouts follow every game, and, from early in the season, they will be targeting key players, many of whom will be offered athletic scholarships. It is accepted that successful high-school performers will be the recipients of such scholarships. For all but the wealthiest of families, this is of vital importance in being able to afford tuition fees and board whilst at university. Outstanding high-school players may be offered scholarships by as many as thirty or forty universities. This is a very competitive process in which the following abuses are not uncommon:

- bribes including offers of cars or girls;
- other forms of cheating (such as altering examination results);
- having 'phantom' students take exams;
- offering jobs to parents of athletes;
- altering high-school transcripts;
- changing admission test scores;
- threatening to bomb the home of a high-school principal who refused to alter transcripts;
- having a coach take an admissions test for a student.

College sport: the middleman

College football was more popular than the professional game until the 1960s, and, although it still receives a disproportionate amount of media and community attention, it now acts as a middleman for those who wish to gain entry to the professional game. The function of college sport is to groom the best young talent, initially recruited from high schools, to toughen them up through a gruelling four years of training, playing and some study and then to filter them into the professional clubs via the annual 'draft'. Since the 1960s, professional clubs have become increasingly reliant on US colleges and universities acting as 'farm teams'.

The best college football and basketball teams generate huge revenues from gate receipts, commercial sponsorship and media fees for their institutions. However, due to anarchic rules linked to a nineteenth-century concept of amateurism, the athletes themselves are forbidden to receive anything other than free tuition, meals and accommodation – which is generally referred to as the scholarship. What the athletes do get, however, is the chance to fulfil an American dream and to have one go at 'making the pros', although, as previously mentioned, this 'dream' becomes reality for only very few.

College sport in the USA is controlled by the National Collegiate Athletic Association (NCAA). This organisation was established in 1906 as the Intercollegiate Athletic Association, primarily to bring order to American football. By 1920, it had taken over the control of all sports at college level and its philosophy was – and to some extent still remains – the Corinthian ideal of producing 'scholar athletes'. There is a considerable amount of pressure on all involved to produce results, and these pressures have created excesses, which, in turn have repeatedly created scandals. The other pressure comes from the fact that college sport has become an entertainment that attracts huge crowds and national media coverage. This not only requires winning teams but also a high level of performance and 'razzamatazz'.

Meanwhile, behind the scenes . . .

As Doyle (1996) suggests, there is another side to collegiate sport. The world of US intercollegiate sport also includes thousands of male and female athletes who compete in relative obscurity in non-revenue-producing sports at large universities along with thousands more ordinary, non-scholarship students at smaller colleges and universities who devote themselves to the sports they love. Many of this latter group add to the development of excellence in the USA since they are often part of teams in the Olympic disciplines which do not have a sufficiently popular following to have a professional arm.

Benefiting from the excellent facilities at most universities and the limited demand on their time for academic study, they can train and prepare for competition on campus. Before the 1990s, this 'student status' was also a means of sidestepping the rules on amateurism that governed Olympic and international athletics. These so-called 'shamateurs' could receive financial aid from commercial companies as long as they were labelled 'academic'. Clearly the system worked, with US Olympic medal tallies over the past half a century or so testament to its success.

Top- level coaching is also a feature of college sport, with institutions employing teams of coaches to prepare their various teams. Cashmore (2000) comments that whilst the players themselves are not allowed to receive any monies apart from their scholarships, many of their coaches typically earn more than top salaried professors and college principals.

Coaches also use college sport as a step ladder to success and will, like the players of whom they have charge, have already cut their teeth in high-school games. Most of the professional coaches in both the NFL and NBA have worked their way up through the school and college sports system.

TABLE 7.1 USA Summer Olympic medals: 1956–2004

Summer Olympic Games

	G	S	B	T
1956	32	25	17	74
1960	34	21	16	71
1964	36	26	28	90
1968	45	28	34	107
1972	33	31	30	94
1976	34	35	25	94
1980				
1984	83	61	30	174
1988	36	31	27	94
1992	37	34	37	108
1996	44	32	25	101
2000	39	26	32	97
2004	36	29	37	102

Coaching pays

American Football's most famous coach, Vince Lombardi, provides a good example of how coaching follows the 'high school–college–professional' pathway:

- Head Coach, New Jersey High School.
- Head Coach, US Military Academy.
- Assistant Head Coach, New York Giants.
- Head Coach, Green Bay Packers.

Coaches also receive a number of other financial and other benefits, often from the booster club (as long as they remain successful). Hart-Nibbrig and Cottingham

(1986) reported that the Head Football Coach of Georgia Institute of Technology received the following benefits:

- his own television show;
- a new Cadillac every six months;
- secretarial and administrative assistance;
- free membership and tabs at private clubs;
- reserved booths of forty seats at stadiums within the state;
- free petrol;
- free motor insurance and speaking honorariums from IBM and General Motors.

The full package amounted to around £500,000 and was in addition to his annual salary paid by the college.

The 'All-American' draft

With the professionalism of football in the 1920s, players who had developed and groomed their skills at university could now make a career out of sport. Cashmore (2000) asserts that this seamless transition from university to professional club has been a feature of American football ever since, with the draft being brought into play in 1936 as a mechanism for equalising the leagues and avoiding an imbalance of power. This annual 'jamboree' in both football and basketball now attracts national attention and is followed closely by both the media and sports fans.

In the same way that colleges and universities select and 'cream off' the best sporting talent from high schools, the process is repeated as professional clubs select and recruit the best college players. Every college game is recorded and analysed by a national office, which scores and ranks every player across the country. It is this system that identifies the best athletes who will go forward into the draft. As previously mentioned, this is the only route into the ranks of the big professional sports and is very elitist, with only a very small percentage of college players getting this far.

In order to retain as level a playing field as possible between the professional teams, the draft works in 'reverse order', with the weakest team from the previous season getting the first pick of the best college athletes. There are a number of rounds to the draft, and there is much trading and competition between teams.

1   What part does school and college sport play in the nurture of elite sports talent in the USA?
2   Why is the scholarship and draft system of the USA classed as elitist?
3   What part does the US government play in the elite sports system in the USA?
4   Explain how the draft system links education and elite sport in the USA.
5   How does elite sport reflect the decentralised administration of sport in the USA?

Texts referred to in this chapter

Bale, J. (1994) *Touchdown to Home Base: Sport in the USA*, Blackwood, South Australia: Altair Publishing.
Cashmore, E. (2000) *Sports Culture: An A–Z Guide*, London and New York: Routledge.
Doyle, A. (1996) 'Intercollegiate Athletics', in D. Levinson and K. Christensen (eds), *Encyclopaedia of World Sport*, Oxford: Oxford University Press, p. 197.
Hart-Nibbrig, N. and Cottingham, C. (1986) *The Political Economy of College Sports*, Lanham, Md.: Lexington Books.

chapter eight

THE GERMAN DEMOCRATIC REPUBLIC

No other nation can match the calculated building of an elite sports network. East Germany was a relatively small country with a population of around 16 million people and yet, for forty years, was at the forefront of international sport. With the development of the Cold War between the East and the West following the Second World War, any cultural activity which could be used to score political points was keenly sought by nations on either side of the political divide. Post-1945, the Communist bloc entered the international sports arena en masse, and Holt (1996) suggests that this was part of a determined effort to show the superiority of the socialist system by breaking as many world records as possible.

Of all the eastern bloc countries, attempts to show political superiority through sport were most apparent in the case of the GDR which, although it could not compete with the post-war economic miracle that was taking place in the Federal Republic (West Germany), discovered that it could use sport as an arm of foreign policy to stress the health, patriotism and superiority of its youth over their counterparts in the decadent West.

Dividing and ruling

In the aftermath of the Second World War, the allies (the USA, the UK, France and the Soviet Union) formed themselves into a European Advisory Commission with the determined aim of eradicating Nazism and politically decentralising the former German state. The Potsdam Agreement, signed in 1945, essentially split Germany into four zones, each administered by control councils and overseen by each of the four allies. This agreement was relatively short-lived and Hardman (1982a) records that the early politics of the Cold War brought about a separation of the USSR-controlled zone from the other three 'western' zones; and this in turn led to the emergence of two separate Germanys.

Whereas West Germany emerged and developed into a liberal so-called Western democratic administration, the eastern part of Germany became firmly orientated towards the Communist ideals of the Soviet Union. This separation was confirmed in 1949 with the promulgation of the *Grundgesetz* or Basic Law which created the Federal Republic of Germany as a social democracy of federal states and was shortly replaced by a Soviet-supported constitution for the eastern zone, which established the Soviet State of Germany or, as it was to be known, the German Democratic Republic.

By 1950, therefore, what had formerly been known as Germany consisted of two separate countries:

- a decentralised administration of ten states in the west;
- a centralised consolidated socialist republic of fifteen administrative units in the east.

From the outset, West Germany retained the major share of the former Germany's industrial base and natural resources and soon recovered from the ravages of the Second World War to become a vibrant and successful global economy. East Germany was geographically much smaller, both in terms of population and industry, relying mainly on agriculture.

Hardman and Naul (2002) suggest that because of its own wartime losses in men and materials, Soviet policy in the immediate post-war period was pretty ruthless. It sought both compensation and revenge through confiscation, dismantlement and demolition, with the consequence that the new East Germany became little more than a Soviet industrial colony. Gradually however, political restrictions were eased, and the GDR was granted more self-control as the political direction of this new state was considered by the Soviet authorities to be in good hands.

Opening the 'shop window'

East Germany was also one of the first countries to recognise the 'shop window' value of sport. It was a country created by politicians with no history or culture and was in need of a vehicle upon which the building of a national identity could be focused. Sport filled this vacuum admirably.

Frustrated by fruitless attempts to gain international recognition through conventional diplomatic channels, the GDR leadership began a persistent campaign to persuade the IOC to acknowledge that this small country had a right to its own flag, national anthem and independent national teams. In successive international sports meetings, the country's exquisitely prepared athletes served as ambassadors in the quest to establish their nation's international sporting status.

However, in 1951, although the IOC officially recognised the Federal Republic of Germany and allowed a team to enter the Helsinki Games of the following year, there was no such invitation for the GDR. In fact, feelings amongst IOC delegates on the East German matter were split into two factions. There were those who argued (as per the Olympic Charter) for bringing together the youth of the world by assisting the two Germanys towards unification, and those who felt that national Olympic committees should not be recognised unless they represented 'regular' states. In the eyes of many, East Germany was simply a 'satellite' of the Soviet Union.

It was not until 1956 that the Soviet Union released East Germany from its status as 'a soviet zone', allowing it to be recognised as a sovereign state and, subsequently, accorded full Olympic status by the IOC. This meant that East Germany could send athletes to both winter and summer games of 1956. There were, however, 'strings' attached . . .

The IOC insisted that both German teams had to compete as one, and only the flag and anthem of the Federal Republic would be recognised. This compromise continued until the winter games of 1968 in Grenoble, when the IOC formally recognised the independent status of both nations.

This change of status was to have its most profound effect at the 1972 Olympic Games in Munich, and Guttmann (1984) suggests that when the East Germans marched into the Munich Olympic Stadium, they had achieved their ultimate objective. They quite literally flaunted their new flag before their Federal Republic hosts, who were required to publicly acknowledge the new-found legitimacy of their eastern neighbour as well as its athletic prowess.

The sporting shop window had been well and truly opened, and the Olympiads of the latter part of the twentieth century provided a platform for both political and sporting ideologies that rapidly led to a wider recognition of the new GDR throughout the world.

Systems of excellence

These 'diplomats in tracksuits' (Hardman and Naul, 2002) needed support and expertise if they were not only to compete at the highest level of international sport but also to do so successfully. This was achieved by means of the development of innovative training programmes and a central institute of elite sport, which remains the model for top-level sports preparation today.

The Deutsche Hochschule für Körperkultur (German College for Body Culture) in Leipzig, founded in 1952, grew into a huge sports complex boasting its own 100,000-seater stadium, boarding schools for pupils of all ages, lecture halls, research institutes and training facilities. Based on a long-term plan for sports excellence, a very thorough system of talent identification and training was developed, which included the measurement (and often X-raying) of all four- to six-year-olds in order to identify sporting potential.

Physical education (or more correctly physical culture) was a compulsory curriculum subject in East German schools. Indeed the country's constitution actually stated its support for this principal subject. Article 18 of the GDR Constitution recognised: 'the contribution of physical education to the all-round physical and intellectual development of the people'. Article 25 guaranteed the right to health preservation and stipulated the measures required in order to apply the principle, such as the promotion of physical culture and school sport.

Though early physical-education syllabuses had a strong military focus, the political demands for sports success at an international level saw a major shift towards sports preparation and training. The so-called 'Three Ts' (training, technique and tactics) began to dominate all school programmes.

Hinsching and Hummel (2002) report that the physical culture syllabus included:

■ versatility in athletic movement;
■ increased intensity of activity;
■ earlier specialisation.

Each session was punctuated by glowing reports of the successes of East German teams and its individual sports stars.

Talent identification

Talent identification was also an integral part of school sport. In the early school years, this formed the first part of the state-sponsored elite sports programme in which every child was screened for sporting potential at the age of seven. Results were recorded and screened by the Central German Gymnastics and Sports Federation (DTSB) based in Berlin. Büch (2002) reports that the Grade 3 performance tests recorded the following details:

- pupil's name;
- date of birth;
- gender;
- demographic details;
- weight;
- height;
- 60m sprint;
- long jump;
- triple jump;
- endurance run;
- rounders ball throw;
- push-ups;
- shot putt;
- a mark for performance in apparatus gymnastics as well as for participation in extra-curricular sport.

These results were screened by government officials in Berlin, and those children who scored well would be invited to attend a local 'training centre' several times a week for up to three years. Their progress at these centres would be carefully monitored, and a decision would be made as to whether they had enough potential to be transferred to a specialist 'children and youths sports school' (KJS).

A network of sports boarding schools, staffed by highly qualified sports coaches and sports-medicine specialists was spread across the country, and students underwent sports-related training for up to twenty hours a week. They were also required to meet high academic standards. Students were continually tested (at an increasingly sophisticated level), with greater emphasis on prognostic testing that focused on innate ability and potential rather than existing levels of ability. The parents of students would also be called in for testing, because the system did not want to waste time and resources on young people who had genetic weaknesses.

Colwin (1992) suggests that the advantage of these sports boarding schools was not simply that they permitted continual monitoring and control of every aspect of the lives of young athletes but also that they provided ideal conditions for training. It was not necessary to travel great distances to twice-daily training sessions or to train very early in the mornings before school. The first training session of the day would take place in the mid-morning during a break in school lessons rather than at an early hour when the athlete's metabolism would not be functioning at anything like optimum level.

Major competitions (Spartakiads) were held at regular intervals in order to help prepare young people for top-level competition in the future. In the run-up to these regional sports finals, students would undergo three to four weeks of intensive training, mirroring the preparation of elite athletes for an Olympic games.

There was also a systematic focus upon the smaller number of sports that the East German authorities had identified in terms of gold-medal potential. These disciplines were identified where there was either a global weakness, due to the small number of nations competing in those sports, or other factors suggesting that there was a high likelihood of medal-winning opportunities. The GDR's greatest successes came in swimming, track and field athletics and gymnastics, with these sports accounting for 70 per cent of the country's Olympic medal tally.

Students who continued to progress at the KJS schools and showed promise at the regional Spartakiads would then graduate to a high-performance sports centre, usually based in and around the state universities. The most famous of these high-performance sports centres was the Research Institute for Physical Culture and Sport based at Leipzig. There were another eight of these centres situated mainly in the major cities of East Germany.

The Leipzig academy was originally set up prior to the Munich Olympic Games of 1972, and it quickly established itself as the model for other centres of sporting excellence. Its major function was to carry out research to identify new methods of training for specific sports that would aid GDR athletes competing at international level.

Following the reunification of Germany in 1990, the centre at Leipzig and the other former GDR elite sports centres formed the initial nucleus of the new German Federal Institutes of Sports Science. It is likely that their legacy in terms of elite sports training and global sports success will continue for some time. However, there is some doubt as to whether the work and (perhaps more importantly) the original philosophy of these centres can continue to exist in the new state of Germany.

By 1990, the Leipzig training centre was in a state of decline, and, although West German officials had been anxious to preserve the scientific aspects of the former East Germany along with its system of training coaches, this had proved difficult to facilitate within the reunified Germany. Such a rigidly centralised system would be difficult to deliver within the framework of a new free and democratic society. Ironically, that very 'freeing of society' has already had a big influence, especially in terms of the freedom of individuals to travel and emigrate to other countries.

Many of the coaches and sports specialists from the former GDR have found a keen market for their skills and knowledge in countries all around the world.

Ten years later (2000) Manfred Ewald, Head of the East German Sports Federation from 1963 to 1988, went on trial in Berlin charged with 142 counts of bodily harm, including charges of administering harmful substances to children at the East German sports schools without their knowledge or that of their parents. Clearly, there were serious ethical and humanitarian issues related to East Germany's short-lived tenure as an Olympic nation. The results of this are given below.

TABLE 8.1 **GDR Summer Olympic medals**

Summer Olympic Games

	G	S	B	T
1956	Joint East/			
	West German			
1960	teams competed			
	at Melbourne,			
1964	Rome and Tokyo			
1968	9	9	7	25
1972	20	23	23	66
1976	40	25	25	90
1980	47	37	42	126
1984	Boycott of LA '84			
1988	37	35	30	102

East German sports example: swimming

The East German sports system, thanks to the authority that came from a philosophy of centralised control, worked closely with education bodies and schools. Swimming was compulsory for all schoolchildren in both second and third grades, and during these lessons, both physical-education staff and state swimming coaches would identify those youngsters who appeared to have talent. Those identified as having potential as swimmers would initially be put into a group that would attend training sessions just once or twice a week. The better swimmers from these groups would eventually be selected to proceed to one of the nine high-performance sports centres. There would normally be around 100 swimmers based at each high-performance centre, the age of entry being eleven for girls and twelve for boys. Most of these young students would receive their education at a nearby state boarding school but would attend the performance centre for their swim-training sessions. Upon entering the programme, swimmers would be given a thorough physical examination and extensive testing of their sports skills. Cichoke (1977) informs us of reports that once accepted into one of these high-performance groups, swimmers would initially train twice a week for two hours per session and would swim a total of 300 kilometres (190 miles) each year.

The 'weeding out' process

After two years of training, those young swimmers who could not swim 100 metres in ninety seconds or faster were weeded out, and the more talented swimmers were pushed up to a higher level of training. Both the duration and the intensity of training would have increased in the space of two years, with between three and five hours training taking place each weekday and two hours on a Saturday. Sunday was a rest day.

At this stage in their young careers, the annual distance covered by most swimmers would have been approximately 1,000 kilometres (600 miles). Colwin (1992) notes that 90 per cent of twelve-year-olds would be 'removed' at the end of their first year.

This monitoring and weeding-out process would continue until the swimmers reached fifteen years of age, at which time they would be moved into the national squad. At this point, they would, in effect, become full-time athletes and would receive all the available support from the state sports bodies. Their continuing status as students ensured that they retained their amateur eligibility.

The training and success of the East German team resulted from the teamwork of groups of highly trained specialists working in close cooperation: coaches, trainers, biochemists, biomechanists, psychologists and physicians. Medical monitoring was an important element in the preparation of elite swimmers (as it was for all other elite performers). Sports scientists would monitor and record swimmers' lactate levels, creatine, oxygen, carbon-dioxide and electrolyte levels at almost every training session. The results of these tests were given to the

70

centre's physician who would analyse the information and then pass on the results to the head coach. Depending on the nature of the report, there would either be an adjustment in the swimmers' workload or appropriate rehabilitative therapy. Many of these results were also sent to the performance headquarters in Leipzig, where government officials and performance directors could track the progress of each swimmer. This information was also used to control each swimmer's diet.

The other great advantage enjoyed by East German swimmers was the use of swimming flumes. The GDR had built six of these swimming treadmills by the 1980s, which outnumbered the total in existence anywhere else in the world. These flumes were used extensively for stroke-technique analysis. The only blight on this 'perfect' model of elite sports preparation was the now common knowledge that many of the swimmers (sometimes not entirely of their own free choice) were using performance-enhancing drugs, particularly steroids.

REVIEW QUESTIONS

1   Why was East Germany's success in sport so special in terms of demography and resources?
2   Explain how and why East Germany used sport as a 'shop window'.
3   What were the key features of the East German elite sports system?
4   Explain how the term 'elitist' can be used to describe the East German sports system.
5   Why were sports such as athletics, swimming and weightlifting specifically targeted by the East German authorities?

Texts referred to in this chapter

Büch, M. (2002) 'Elite Sport', in K. Hardman and R. Naul, *Sport and Physical Education in Germany*, London and New York: Routledge.

Cichoke, A. (1977) 'The German Democratic Republic's Planned Dominance of the 1980 Olympics', *Swimming Technique*, 14 (3): 81–5.

Colwin, C. M. (1992) *Swimming into the 21st Century*, Human Kinetics.

Guttmann, A. (1984) *The Games Must Go On: Avery Brundage and the Olympic Movement*, New York: Columbia University Press.

Hardman, K. (1982a) 'The Development of PE in West Germany 1981', *Physical Education Review*, 4 (1): 46–60.

Hardman, K. (1982b) 'The development of physical education in the GDR, 1980', *Physical Education Review* 5 (1): 45.

Hardman, K. and Naul, R. (2002) *Sport and Physical Education in Germany*, London and New York: Routledge, 2002.

Hinsching, J. and Hummel, A. (eds) (2002) 'Schulsportforschung *in* Ostdeutschland, 1945–90', in K. Hardman and R. Naul, *Sport and Physical Education in Germany*, London and New York: Routledge, pp. 9–13.

Holt, R. (1996) 'Patriotism', in D. Levinson and K. Christensen (eds), *Encyclopaedia of World Sport*, Oxford: Oxford University Press, p. 293.

chapter nine

WORLD CLASS AT LONG LAST
UK sport excellence, 2000+

'We need to learn the lessons of our competitor nations and have the most professional system for talent development and support of excellence.'

Tony Blair (2000)

The new UK Sport (formerly the Sports Council) programme, initiated in the spring of 1999 and developed with the Department of Culture, Media and Sport and the four home sports councils is made up of two new policies:

1   UK Sport Institute (UKSI) Network: ten regional centres in England with separate national centres in Scotland, Wales and Northern Ireland;
2   World Class Performance Programme: funds performance and subsistence costs of UK elite athletes (money comes from the Lottery Sports Fund via the athletes' home sports council).

The philosophy and aims of the two programmes are reflected in the statements issued at the launch of the new initiative in March 1999:

'The establishment of a network of world class facilities is crucial if we are to provide the right framework within which our top and aspiring sportsmen and women can train and compete more successfully' and 'Quite simply we believe [the new policies] are essential if we are to win more medals. We are launching the network on the back of the latest thinking, data and research from around the world'; and 'The network will assist governing bodies and their top performers to reach their targets in terms of championships and medals. Using a state of the art approach, a comprehensive network of services and facilities will be

73

available, with each outlet taking the lead in supporting the delivery of excellence in sport with the best sports scientists, medical professionals, coaches and support personnel.'

(Trevor Brooking, Chair, Sport England, March 1999;
UKSI Press Release, March 1999)

UK sport has recognised, as a result of a comparative study of successful sports nations, the need to invest in young talented performers from an early age. Only if the most talented individuals are fully supported can they be expected to fulfil their potential and excel on the world's sporting stage.

Programmes of excellence across the UK are coordinated at UKSI headquarters in London. The main role is to monitor and assess the quality of the service and facilities offered to both sports and athletes across the network. UKSI also coordinates research and development and ensures that focus is placed upon those priorities which are identified by participating sports. It also ensures that developments around the world are monitored and that programmes based on developments thought to be appropriate for application in the UK are made available to athletes and sports bodies here.

A UKSI board oversees the running of the network and consists of a number of senior sports stars, coaches and administrators, including Sir Steve Redgrave and Steve Cram. The board has been given the task of developing a coordination of policy and programmes for the various branches of the UKSI. They will review the work of these centres on a regular basis.

The UKSI headquarters also coordinates and manages the following programmes:

- Elite Coach Education Programme: this initiative, jointly developed with Sports Coach UK and the BOA aims to meet the needs of coaches in the 'world-class' environment. Coaches identified by the performance director in each sport are offered a range of training courses and resources to aid in their coaching education.
- ACE UK – Athlete Career and Education Services – based on the Australian model and currently headed by the AIS former ACE director: the aim of this programme is to enhance an athlete's personal development and sporting performance. This will be done through access to individualised support to help athletes cope with their lives as elite athletes and also to help prepare them for life after sport. Athletes can access services including career advice, educational support, personal finance training, media- and presentation-skills training.

A range of personal-development courses are delivered by the ACE programme:

- basic and advanced media training;
- seeking sponsorship;
- personal image and presentation;
- effective time management;
- interview skills;
- job-seeking skills;
- budgeting and financial planning;
- personal taxation for athletes;
- stress management;
- nutritional cooking;
- The 'Success in Athens' programme (previously 'Success in Sydney' in 1999) – aimed specifically at providing additional support for the UK's best athletes aiming to compete at the next Olympics and Paralympics.

In order to benefit from this additional support, the athletes and teams must have demonstrated real potential to win medals and have a proven track record of success at world-championship level. The funding is being used to provide specific equipment, sports-science medicine and training aids such as altitude simulators.

There are currently members of staff at the UKSI London headquarters with expertise in areas such as coaching, athlete liaison, sports science, sports medicine, research analysis, technology and innovation, IT, education and training.

UKSI national network centres

In practice, the network centres will act as a coordinating mechanism to harness the services in the region in which they are situated, and there will be a number of smaller specialised centres in each region. There are currently thirteen national network centres delivering excellence programmes across the UK:

1	East	Bedford
2	East Midlands	Loughborough University/Holme Pierrepont
3	North	Gateshead International Stadium
4	North-west	Sports City, Manchester
5	South	Bisham Abbey
6	South Coast	Southampton University
7	South East	Crystal Palace
8	South West	University of Bath

9	West Midlands	Lilleshall
10	Yorkshire	Don Valley Stadium
11	**UKSI Scotland**	University of Stirling
12	**UKSI Northern Ireland**	University of Ulster, Jordanstown Campus
13	**UKSI Wales**	Welsh Insitute of Sport, Cardiff

The primary role of each network centre is to assist national governing bodies and their top performers as identified through the World-Class programme to reach their targets in terms of championships and medals. This will be achieved by providing both athletes and coaches with a comprehensive network of services at each centre, which, in turn, will bring together the best sports scientists, medical professionals and support personnel and provide them with a base from which to work. The network centres will also act as a vehicle for accessing an overseas network of facilities and services, including warm-weather training, acclimatisation, altitude and winter-sport venues.

A national sailing centre will also be completed at Weymouth in 2004. This £7 million facility, which is jointly funded by the National Lottery and the Regional Development Agency, will provide elite sailors with a training base as well as opening up sailing opportunities for the local community.

The 'World Class' programme

This programme invests 'World Class' funds to achieve consistent success in top-level international competitions such as the Olympic Games, Paralympics and World Deaf Games.

Teams and individuals on the 'World Class' programme meet agreed selection criteria before being nominated by their respective governing bodies. There are three stages of the programme, and the amount of support and funding increases as athletes move towards the 'World Class' performance level.

1   World Class Performance: for the training and preparation of elite performers with the potential to win medals within a time scale of six years.
2   World Class Potential: the development of performers with the potential to win medals within the next ten years.
3   World Class Start: identifies and nurtures those performers who can achieve future world-class success, e.g., new football academies.

In the restructure of elite sport in the UK in February 2006, the three levels of the programme were renamed: World Class Podium, World Class Development and World Class Talent.

Houlihan and White (2002) report that whereas the National Lottery has provided the resources for elite development, the World Class Performance programmes have provided the specific policy infrastructure. Most significantly, the World Class Performance grants awarded via the governing bodies have allowed athletes to cover their living expenses whilst training, a recognition that to compete at the highest levels UK athletes need to devote themselves to training on a full-time basis.

The World Class Performance programme was soon complemented by other schemes, including World Class Potential (1998), designed to provide systematic and well-resourced support to those responsible for identifying and nurturing talented young people. World Class Start (1998) completed the 'World Class' programmes with funding to help national governing bodies to search more systematically for young talent and to develop appropriate coaching systems and techniques.

World Class Performance Programme

This programme ensures that lottery funding is targeted at the UK's top sportsmen and women. The programme is special because, unlike other lottery-funded projects, it provides direct funding to people rather than facilities and buildings. The fund is given to:

- the four home sports councils
- the British Paralympic Association
- National Governing Bodies
- any athlete in the world Top 20.

Funding consists of two parts:

1   Funding awarded to governing bodies to cover support services to athletes, e.g., coaching and medical staff, warm-weather training and sports science.
2   Athlete personal awards: awarded to athletes to help with day-to-day living and sporting costs. The average grant (in 2003) is £10,000–12,000.

Currently (2003) the UK Sport World Class Performance Programme supports twenty-four sports and 730 athletes with a budget of around £20 million a year. This funding is, however, totally dependent upon members of the public purchasing tickets for the twice-weekly lottery draws.

Case study: East Midlands National Network Centre

Loughborough University has been chosen to be part of the English Institute of Sport, which, in turn, will work closely with the other home-country networks and the UK Institute of Sport. The institutes are charged with supporting those sports performers and their coaches who are working at the very highest level, or have the potential to do so. Loughborough University and Sport England are developing a package of sports facilities (athletics, badminton, gymnastics, hockey, netball and swimming) to supplement the already extensive resources.

As a regional institute of sport, the facility is required to offer the following mandatory services to athletes in their region in addition to generic support facilities:

- acclimatisation accommodation;
- conditioning suites;
- sports massage;
- physiotherapy.

(Sports-medicine rooms, sport-science labs, etc., are currently being developed on site.)

Simultaneously, the core personnel and the expertise within the university, the region and the sports themselves will be identified to enable a coordinated programme of the highest level. This team will link with staff in facilities which are being developed throughout the region. Linking with other educational establishments and employment options will ensure that the broader needs of performers are met.

National governing bodies are continuing to develop programmes of excellence and talent identification. The English Hockey Association (EHA), for example, is currently introducing a programme of player assessment at 'World Class Start' Level for under-fifteen, under-sixteen, under-seventeen and under-eighteen age-groups, after which players will be invited to attend national assessment camps and extended periods of training at the regional academies throughout the year. Once players reach the top level, they become eligible for nomination by the EHA for World Class Performance funding, which, in 2002, supported forty-eight elite level players (twenty-four men and twenty-four women) with £15,000 per year and a further forty-eight players with a smaller amount of £2,000–3,000.

The revised finding figures released by UK Sport in their plan for the 2012 Olympics included the following awards:

The English Institute of Sport (EIS) has developed a priority list of sports in order to maximise the effect of its work. It will be reviewed annually with changes made and published each December. The information below is therefore subject to change.

Premier sports
Sports considered important to England but which have a significant professional element:

- cricket
- football
- golf
- rugby league
- rugby union
- tennis

These sports receive
- negotiated access to priority services based on financial need. Provision of other services will be made on a cost recovery basis.

The UKSI Athlete Medical Scheme automatically covers all athletes from Priority 1 and 2 sports. This package is tailored to meet athletes' needs and as well as providing easy access to services will also help in the analysis of injury, treatment and rehabilitation. In total around 700 athletes each year are covered by the scheme, which is directed by the UKSI and managed through the BOA.

Priority 1 sports
Sports consistently winning medals at Olympic, Paralympic or World Championship levels:

- athletics
- cycling
- rowing
- sailing
- squash

These sports receive:
- priority use of EIS facilities, primary and supplementary services;
- use of full-time EIS staff for national camps and team activities.

Priority 2 sports
Sports with recent medal successes or the potential to do so at Olympic, Paralympic or World Championship levels:

- badminton
- bobsleigh/Skeleton
- boxing
- canoeing
- diving
- equestrian
- gymnastics
- hockey
- judo
- netball
- modern pentathlon
- rugby union (women)
- shooting
- swimming
- triathlon
- water skiing

These sports receive:
- full access to primary services and one other: e.g., psychology
- negotiated use of EIS staff for national team activities.

Priority 3 sports
Individual or small groups of athletes identified as potential medallists

- archery
- ice/speed skating
- karate
- orienteering
- power lifting

These sports receive negotiated use of services for performance athletes and governing bodies.

FIGURE 9.1 EIS priority sports.

Olympic/Paralympic Podium Programme – most money will go to those sports most likely to bring back medals, funding £70,000 an athlete (the athletes themselves will only receive around £23,930 – the rest of the money will be used to fund support for the athlete such as coaching, physiotherapy and training costs).

Olympic/Paralympic Performance Programme – six years from podium positions. Funding at £38,000 an athlete – again the athlete will only receive around a third of this.

Talent ID and Confirmation Programme – eight years from podium. Funding at £48,000 an athlete – again the athlete will only receive around a third of this.

The other 'Home' Institutes

Scottish Institute of Sport

Set up by SportScotland in 1998, the Scottish Institute of Sport (see Figure 9.2) is funded by the SportScotland Lottery fund and caters for over 200 athletes from a wide range of sports. The main site was initially in Edinburgh but moved to the University of Stirling in the autumn of 2000. This purpose-built facility acts as a hub, as is the case with the English network, and operates as the central base for a network of six centres, each of which is responsible for identifying and nurturing sports talent in their own region.

The six institutes are:

1 Central Scotland
2 East of Scotland
3 Grampian
4 Highland
5 Tayside and Fife
6 West of Scotland.

SCOTTISH INSTITUTE OF SPORT

FIGURE 9.2
The Scottish Institute of Sport logo.

In addition, both the Scottish Institute of Sport and the area institutes form part of the UK-wide network, thus ensuring that Scottish athletes have access to the very best support, wherever in the UK they are based. A Scottish athlete studying at an English university can access the nearest UKSI network centre and continue to receive 'World Class' support.

Athletes selected to receive institute support have tailored programmes to help them develop as world-class athletes. Dedicated programmes in coaching (including training and competition programmes), technical support, sports medicine, sports science, performance analysis and athlete career and education (ACE UK) are all made available to athletes within these programmes.

There are nine core sports in the Scottish Institute network:

- athletics
- badminton
- curling
- football
- golf
- hockey
- judo
- rugby
- swimming.

Additionally, the very top Scots performers in other sports have been identified to be part of the institute and its programme as individual athletes.

The area institutes of sport networks offer potentially successful athletes access to top quality coaching programmes delivered by experienced and highly qualified coaches. This includes access to the best training facilities in their region and a fully integrated and personally tailored strength and conditioning programme for each individual athlete. The area institute also provides sports science support including fitness assessment, sports psychology and sports-nutrition advice. Sports medicine and physiotherapy support is also available at each area institute as well as ACE programmes and courses. Only selected athletes receive this support from the area institutes, and a Scottish Institute selection policy has been agreed between the institute, national governing bodies and SportScotland. The policy states that to be selected athletes must:

- be eligible to compete for Scotland and be committed to do so;
- have the potential to be a Scottish Institute athlete in the future;
- be identified by their national governing body against a nationally agreed benchmark;

- be able to benefit from inclusion in area institute programmes;
- live, work or train within the geographical area of the selecting area institute;
- have the potential to win at British, European, Commonwealth, World, Olympic or Paralympic level at either age group or senior level;
- be identified as an athlete with the greatest potential not already supported through the Scottish and area institute network.

UKSI Cymru

This is a network of services offered to athletes in Wales and is coordinated by the Sports Council for Wales (see Figure 9.3). It provides athletes with world-class facilities, sports science, sports medicine and lifestyle support. As elsewhere in the UK, the institute operates through a network of sites with the Welsh Institute of Sport, based at Sophia Gardens in Cardiff, acting as the hub. Other main sites include:

- National Indoor Athletics Arena at University of Wales Institute, Cardiff;
- Plas Menai National Water Sports Centre in North Wales;
- Welsh National Swimming Pool in Swansea;
- Cricket School of Excellence in Cardiff;
- Welsh National Cycling Velodrome, Newport.

The Welsh Institute of Sport at Sophia Gardens has been established for over thirty years and became part of the UKSI network in 1998. The centre caters for sixteen sports and is the only UK centre to hold BOA accreditation as a training centre for judo, table tennis and badminton. The facility also provides accommodation for around sixty athletes and coaches as well as a range of training and fitness facilities. Most of the sports-science and sports-medicine service is

FIGURE 9.3
The Welsh Institute of Sport logo.

world class at long last

provided by the national indoor arena where the main focus sport is athletics. This is one of the few UK venues with a 200-metre indoor track and indoor training and competitive facilities for all field events.

The most modern element of the network is the new national pool, which was opened in March 2003. Constructed as an extension to the existing University Sports Centre, the pool was funded mainly by lottery money and is supported and managed jointly by the City and County of Swansea and the University of Wales College, Swansea. The lottery investment of £8.5 million (total cost £10.7 million) was the largest lottery award for sport in Wales. The National Lottery Panel has insisted that the priority usage of this new facility should be for performance swimmers at national level with more than twenty-four hours of pool time per week being made available to the National Centre Squad.

Plas Menai National Watersports Centre was a pre-existing national sports centre, having been purpose built in 1980. The centre is owned by the Sports Council for Wales and offers the widest range of water sports activities in the UK. In addition to training and competition facilities for top-level performers, the centre also offers specialist coach-training programmes and a range of educational courses. It is also the headquarters of the Welsh Yachting Association.

Sports Institute Northern Ireland (SINI)

Sports Institute Northern Ireland (SINI) is based at Jordanstown and is a partner-ship between the Sport Council for Northern Ireland and the University of Ulster (see Figure 9.4). SINI aims to provide specialist services and key facilities for up to 110 able-bodied and disabled, international and national sportsmen and women to improve their competitive capacity.

Over £12 million has been invested in the project on the University of Ulster site that includes:

- an indoor training centre;
- athletics training track;
- sports-medicine facilities;
- strength and conditioning facility;
- playing pitches.

The institute is jointly funded by:

- the Sports Council for Northern Ireland;
- the University of Ulster.

FIGURE 9.4
The Sports
Institute
Northern
Ireland logo.

The institute provides the nucleus of top-quality training and support services, available primarily at the University of Ulster's Jordanstown campus, and has established formal links with other key facilities nearby. The Institute's stated core purpose is, 'to create an environment that nurtures and leads elite athletes and coaches through the provision of facilities, services and expertise' (SINI web site, 2003). Its long-term goal is to produce 'consistent medal winning performances', which will be achieved through three strategic goals:

1   supporting winning athletes and their coaches;
2   creating world-class training facilities;
3   communicating successfully.

Initially, a six-month trial monitored the progress of fifty-seven athletes in four core sports who were given full access to the institute ands its services. The aim was to monitor the athlete services and commitment of athletes to an institute environment. Following this successful pilot programme, the institute is being expanded in terms of both the number of athletes and the range of sports it can cater for as funding becomes available.

Services provided to elite athletes at SINI include:

- strength and conditioning advice support and programme development;
- sports medicine;
- physiotherapy/injury management;
- sport science, including physiology, nutrition, biomechanics, sports psychology and performance analysis;
- performance lifestyle (formerly ACE service);
- high-performance planning.

REVIEW QUESTIONS

1 Describe the two key elements of the current elite sport programme in the UK.
2 What is the function/role of the ACE UK programme?
3 What is the philosophy/thinking behind the creation of a network of sports institutes across the country?
4 Explain the type of support a UKSI centre can offer to an elite performer preparing for top-level competition.
5 What has been the main source of funding for the development of the current elite sports system in the UK?
6 Describe the three elements of the World Class programme.
7 Explain the ways in which different sports access the UKSI network.
8 How do the national institutes of Scotland, Wales and Northern Ireland compare with the English centres?
9 What influence do the national governing bodies of sport have in the elite sports system?
10 How has the UK adapted current elite sports systems from other cultures?

Text referred to in this chapter

Houlihan, B. and White, A. (2002) *The Politics of Sports Development*, London and New York: Routledge.

chapter ten

WIN AT ALL COSTS?
The art of gamesmanship

'Given the amount of money at stake in professional sports it's hardly surprising that many competitors are prepared to do what it takes by fair means or foul to get the desired result.'

Cashmore (1996: 170)

Sport has its rules, and 'deviance' occurs when participants break or attempt to break these rules. We call much of this 'deviance' cheating.

The main concern at present is the apparent rise in the different forms of cheating in sports – e.g., drug abuse, bribing of officials and the kind of 'technological cheating' that occurs in sports such as Formula 1 motor racing. Cheating is not, however, a new concept. We know that the Olympians of ancient times took 'tonics' to try to increase their performances. Some might argue that cheating is an important element of sport – without which sport would be dull.

This need to win at the games of ancient times is noted by Tomlinson and Whannel (1984), who state that competitors strived for 'either the wreath or death' – for victory alone brought glory for those ancient athletes. Finishing positions other than those of the victors were rarely recorded, since defeat brought undying shame. There were no team events at those games, since no individual athlete wanted to share the glory of victory. Many of the events were extremely violent. The combative events – the most popular spectacles – were concluded with little concern for safety or fairness. There were no weight categories to equalise strength or size, no round sand, no ring . . . bouts were essentially fights to the finish. Since death was one of the recognised risks, athletic fatalities were not regarded as murder in Ancient Greece.

Sporting values

The sporting philosophy that emerged from English public schools and universities of the nineteenth and early twentieth centuries had a very different focus. The ethics of fair play and sportsmanship was central to the concept of rational sport.

Sport relies on sportsmanship, people conforming to the written and unwritten rules of sport. The notion of fair play requires that the opponent be treated as an equal and, although the intention is to be victorious, this can only be done by adherence to the rules and a code of conduct developed through sporting tradition. This includes such niceties as shaking hands and cheering the other team from the field at the end of the game. Sportsmanship puts team before individual and so team spirit is paramount, a product of the intense interhouse sporting competitions that evolved in the great English public schools in the latter part of the nineteenth century (see Plate 10.1).

To cheat not only destroys the game but also detracts from any personal achievement. A win gained by cheating is a hollow victory, because, although extrinsic rewards may be gained, the more fulfilling intrinsic ones will not. This concept of fair play fitted well with the state of the political and economic developments of the world at the time. Dobbs (1973) discusses this new view of sport and how it grew in strength in parallel with the development of British imperialism. The games, and especially the virtues and values associated with them, corresponded with what was perceived to be required for success in the

PLATE 10.1
The concept of sportsmanship was popularised in the nineteenth century by English public schools.

Illustration: British Library 12810.cc.39

outside world. Dash, daring, loyalty, courage and endurance . . . all of these qualities, fostered on the sports field, were at a premium in wars against hostile tribes who lacked weapons and organisation; a world of endless new frontiers and the challenges that came with them.

Times change

Is this concept of fair play outdated? It certainly remains an important part of British sport, but for many performers today, the overriding desire is to win – at all costs if necessary. World governing bodies such as FIFA try to foster sportsmanship by promoting 'Fair Play' awards, but many feel that today's materialistic values constantly promoted by an increasingly global media make this battle a hard one to win. It is interesting to note that in the 1990 World Cup finals, England had the honour of winning the Fair Play Award but only reached the semi-final – perhaps reinforcing the American cliché that 'nice guys finish last'.

There is, however, plenty of evidence to suggest that the commonly held view of sportsmanship and fair play being the cornerstones of Edwardian sport might be a little wide of the truth. It would appear that in the early twentieth century, when most modern sports were evolving, the need to win was equally as important. Kristy (1995) reports that the London Olympics in 1908 were marred by what was largely considered to be 'anti-American/pro-British' judging by the (mainly British) officials. In the 400 metres, the British were sure that their man could win but feared the Americans, who, it was said, had prepared for the games in a most unsporting manner. Most of the US team were students who had spent the previous year training for the games.

During the race, British judges stood at 20-yard intervals around the track to spot any technical errors the Americans might make. Although there were no lane markings and no apparent physical contact between any of the runners, the judges considered that the American J. C. Carpenter had 'run wide' and blocked Britain's Wyndham Halswelle when he tried to pass him. The judges stepped on to the track, broke the winning tape and declared the race void. Carpenter was disqualified from the rematch, for which lanes *were* marked, and two other Americans withdrew from the race in protest.

There was further disagreement in the tug of war, where the rules clearly stated that only 'everyday footwear' could be worn. When the British team appeared wearing boots with steel rims, the Americans complained but were overruled and, again, withdrew from the competition in protest.

The founder (President of the Olympic Movement) Baron de Coubertin viewed these conflicts as valuable and that they added interest to sport.

Gamesmanship or just plain cheating?

The alternative philosophy to sportsmanship is referred to as 'gamesmanship'. This implies that whatever means available might be used to overcome an opponent. If this can be done without breaking rules (or possibly bending them a little), fine; if not, the only aim here is to win, and, for many, it becomes not a question of 'bending' the rules to one's advantage but driving a cart and horses through them if necessary. Stephen Potter published his book *The Theory and Practice of Gamesmanship* as long ago as 1947, so clearly the occurrence of such practices is not solely the domain of today's sporting stars.

Many sports stars of rather more recent times might be classed as 'gamesmen' or 'manipulators'. Former tennis star John McEnroe would disrupt the concentration of his opponents by arguing with and abusing himself, the umpire and the crowd.

Gamesmanship has now gained varying degrees of acceptability in the modern sporting world and encompasses moralities that extend from 'we shall [intend to] play fairly' to 'win at all costs'. Sadly, the ever-growing pressure to win and the potential rewards for doing so often mean that those performers adopt an attitude of 'if you can't beat 'em, join 'em' in respect of bending rules to their own advantage.

Just 'not cricket'!

A more recent publication also shatters the generally held belief that the essentially 'English' game of cricket has always been above such questionable considerations. Rae (2001) claims that although there were times and places, particularly in the 1950s and 1960s, when cricket was played more or less honestly, the kind of racist remarks doled out in the 1957 tourist match between Surrey and the West Indies would nowadays result in police charges – and certainly will not be reproduced here!

Rae reminds us that the modern-day notion of Victorian cricketers providing some kind of superior model of conduct is, largely speaking, pretty wide of the mark. He also points out that in the days before pads, gloves and boxes (not to mention funny helmets), the game was genuinely life-threatening. Those who saw the late Hansie Cronje's match-fixing as 'shabby behaviour' should remember that cricket originally grew in popularity precisely because of gambling.

Aussies to stop 'sledging'

In the almost manufactured morality that pervades much of modern-day sport, the Australian cricketers began the 2003/4 season by asserting that 'sledging' (the verbal intimidation of opposition players) was a separate issue to the art of gamesmanship. 'What you won't see is sledging. What you will see is games-manship' said Australian cricketer Andrew Symonds at the launch of the Australian domestic season.

Another aspect of gamesmanship is the 'hype' that surrounds the build-up to an event. Primarily generated by and for the advantage of the media, this approach is also used by competitors to 'out-psych' or intimidate their opponents.

Polley (1998) discusses at length the way in which both media and sports organisations in the UK often use military vocabulary and historical events. He details the approach to the 1990 World Cup semi-final match between England and West Germany, which was seen by the media as a re-run of both the 1966 World Cup final and two world wars. Headlines in the UK press included 'Achtung! Surrender: For You Fritz, Ze Championship Is Over' (*Daily Mirror*) and 'Let's Blitz Fritz' (*The Sun*).

Dheensaw and Binder (1996) suggest that the pressure to win can be so great that some nations or individuals will do just about anything to get a precious Olympic gold medal. At the 1976 Montreal games, modern pentathlete Boris Onishenko of the Soviet Union came in as a gold and silver medallist from two previous Olympics but proved to be a poor electrician. He had tampered with his epee and created an electrical switch which allowed him to register 'hits' on the official scoring equipment . . . hits that he was not really making. He was found out, disqualified from the competition and sent home in disgrace. Why someone who had already won an Olympic gold medal should feel the need to cheat in this way is open to debate. Perhaps it was simply that he needed to be on top and knew that he was past his best – or that life back home in the USSR would be rather less agreeable for a 'has-been'.

The better-known example of Canadian sprinter Ben Johnson seemed to carry a more obvious motive: wealth. Johnson was expected to make between 10 and 15 million dollars by being the fastest man on the planet. Although a top-class sprinter, he still felt the need to use anabolic steroids, failed a drugs test following his victory at the games of 1988, was stripped off his medal and was banned from athletics – initially for four years. Following a subsequent reinstatement and further offences, Johnson was banned for life. Two other medallists, Carl Lewis and Linford Christie both passed drugs tests at the games but were also later banned for drug violations.

This might suggest that drug abuse is a major problem in elite sprinting. Indeed, further allegations at the time of the Lewis case suggested that there was an extensive cover-up undertaken by US sports authorities to hide the fact that a number of US Olympic athletes had failed drugs tests. In 2003, the discovery of tests to identify the drug Tetrahydrogestrinone (THG) showed that there are still those who are prepared to bend the rules in the fervent hope that they can do so without being caught.

'Foul play'

Modern sport has a growing problem of violence, and in some sports, traditional and mutual respect between opponents may have disappeared. In rugby union, we have seen practices such as 'stamping' and deliberately kicking an opponent on the floor, which often requires the victim to leave the field of play. In football, the quick-footed striker or clever mid-field player is a prime target, and in all the above instances, the more damage that is inflicted, the more effective a defence or individual defender is considered to have been. In American football, the aim of the defence is to 'sack the quarterback', whilst in rugby it is the tactically aware fly half who warrants 'special attention'. Without key players, the opposition threat is considerably reduced, and such approaches are becoming more and more commonplace and (sadly) almost as acceptable.

Again, there appears to be a link between increasing violence in sport and money. In association football, the so-called 'professional foul' makes a clear reference to the perceived difference between the old amateur and professional codes. In the 'professional foul', the attacker is deliberately knocked down to prevent him scoring – even though this may result in a penalty. There is at least a chance that the goalkeeper might save that.

Various forms of deviant behaviour are a response to ever-increasing rewards. The 'win-ethic' decrees that the result justifies the means used to achieve it. This may include resorting to illegal practices, either during competition or whilst in training. Such problems increase as less capable performers are influenced by and attempt to copy the practices of their heroes as seen in the press or on their television screens. Cashmore argues that there is already considerable evidence supporting the suggestion that if athletes are known and seen to use drugs of any kind, then young people may be encouraged to follow.

REVIEW QUESTIONS

1 Give three different examples of how people can cheat in a chosen sport.
2 Suggest three reasons why people cheat in sport.
3 Why is winning by cheating considered a hollow victory?
4 Explain what is meant by the term 'sportsmanship'.
5 How does the meaning of the term 'gamesmanship' differ?
6 Discuss the historical background and the evolution of sportsmanship at the turn of the twentieth century.
7 Explain, using examples, what is meant by the term 'professional foul'.
8 Discuss the negative effect that cheating by elite sports performers can have on grass-roots sport.
9 Why can violence in sport be viewed as an historical issue?
10 How can sports bodies attempt to promote fair play in their competitions?

Texts referred to in this chapter

Cashmore, E. (1996) *Making Sense of Sports*, 2nd edn, London and New York: Routledge.

Coubertin, P. (1977) 'The Fourth Olympiad 1908', *Olympic Review* 114 (April): 248–52.

Dheensaw, C. and Binder, D. (1996) *Celebrate the Spirit: The Olympic Games*, Victoria, BC: Orca.

Dobbs, B. (1973) *Edwardians at Play: Sport 1890–1914*, London: Pelham Books.

Kristy, D. (1995) *Coubertin's Olympics: How the Games Began*, Minneapolis, Minn.: Lerner Publications.

Money, T. (1997) *Manly and Muscular Diversions*, London: Duckworth.

Polley, M. (1998) *Moving the Goalposts*, London and New York: Routledge.

Potter, S. (1947) *The Theory and Practice of Gamesmanship*, London: Hart-Davis.

Rae, S. (2001) *It's Not Cricket: A History of Skulduggery, Sharp Practice and Downright Cheating in the Noble Game*, London: Faber & Faber.

Tomlinson, A. and Whannel, G. (1984) *Five Ring Circus: Money, Power and Politics at the Olympic Games*, London: Pluto Press.

chapter eleven

CITIUS, ALTIUS, FORTIUS, PHARMACUS
Drugs in elite sport

Drug-taking in sport is not, of course, a modern-day phenomenon. Evidence suggests that the ancient Greeks took hallucinogenic extracts from mushrooms in order to enhance their performance at the ancient Olympics and, along with the Egyptians and Romans, had regular recourse to opium.

Chemically active derivatives of plants have wide-ranging applications, many of which could be used to aid athletic performance. Mars (1996) suggests that as new drugs and natural hormones have become available, they have rapidly been assimilated into the sporting sphere.

Cashmore reports that, within sport, we know little of the systematic application of stimulants, though after 1879 when six-day cycle races began in Europe, riders favoured ether and caffeine to delay the onset of fatigue. Sprint cyclists used nitroglycerine, a chemical later used in conjunction with heroin, cocaine, strychnine and others to make 'speed balls' which were given to horses before races in the 1930s. Thomas J. Hicks, winner of the 1904 Olympic marathon, also used the highly poisonous stimulant strychnine.

Ephedrine (the forerunner of amphetamines) was developed during the 1930s, and their first known use in sport occurred at the 1936 Olympics. During the post-war period, their popularity increased, with the Danish Cyclist, Knut Jensen, becoming the first Olympic drug fatality during the 100-kilometre time trial of the Rome Olympiad of 1960. Perhaps more well known to sports enthusiasts in the UK was the death during the 1967 Tour de France of English cyclist Tommy Simpson on the slopes of Mont Ventoux.

Although French physiologist Ernest Laqueur succeeded in isolating the male hormone testosterone in 1935, it was not until the 1950s and 1960s that American athletes and footballers began experimenting with drugs such as anabolic steroids as the pressures to perform increased and the need for physical power became a key feature of their sports.

Scott (1971) reported that investigations concerning one US college football team showed that a quarter of the team had used steroids. He also refers to athletes at the 1968 Olympics openly discussing the practical use of drugs. In a survey by American Magazine *Sports Illustrated* (1983), it was estimated that between 40 and 90 per cent of all college football players were using steroids.

The most recent and potentially dangerous developments in doping practices include growth hormones, blood doping involving transfusions of an athlete's own blood and erythropoietin (EPO). With all these substances and practices, there is considerable risk to those who undertake them. We are no longer concerned with 'one-off' pills and potions but the long-term chemical altering of the make-up of human beings in order that they might win gold medals.

Drug abuse has been one of the main areas of deviant activity in sport in recent decades. It is not clear whether the actual level of drug-taking has gone up or whether we are now simply more aware of such practices because testing systems have improved. It is also very difficult to decide where the line should be drawn between legal and illegal substances. Many athletes have returned positive tests but claim that all they took was a cough mixture or other everyday product which can be bought over the counter at any pharmacy.

The ultimate in gamesmanship

Drug-taking is the ultimate in gamesmanship: taking something to enhance your performance and increase your chances of winning. There is a range of performance-enhancing drugs that athletes may take. Most of them, however, originated as genuine medical treatments, and it is their 'other beneficial effects' which have been utilised by athletes in order to improve their athletic performance illegally.

The range and availability of these types of drug is constantly on the increase, with some substances now being either artificially manufactured or being 'tweaked' by chemists. This makes control very difficult.

Official estimates suggest that one in ten athletes on the world stage are using drugs to aid their sporting performance. Others, such as Olympic silver medallist and convicted steroid-trader David Jenkins, argue that as many as 50 per cent of active track-and-field athletes have used drugs at some time during their careers.

The huge increases in potential rewards for winning may have made the temptation to take drugs too great for many athletes to resist. Ben Johnson clearly felt the risk was worthwhile. Even though he was stripped of his 1988 gold medal

drugs in elite sport

and banned from competition (eventually for life), he continued to make money from his fame.

Cashmore (1996) suggests that reasons for this rise in drug-taking are to be found in cultural changes: as the need to achieve excellence in sports has increased, so the back-up teams for performers have become bigger and bigger. All top-level athletes now have a medical team working with them. Drugs are simply one of a number of elements that figure in the preparation of an elite athlete. Messner (1992) is of the opinion that the 'win-at-all-costs' ethic has permeated sport at the highest level and that this has increased the likelihood of some performers turning to performance-affecting drugs.

Most media attention has been focused on the use of steroids. These artificial male hormones allow the performer to train harder and longer and to recover more quickly from heavy training loads than would otherwise be possible. They have been difficult to trace until relatively recently as they are not in themselves performance-enhancing drugs.

Athletes take steroids in the closed season during the heaviest period of training. A breakthrough in detection of these drugs came with the testing of athletes at any time during the year, which meant that for the first time illegal out-of-season activity could be detected. Recent developments in the detection of previously untraceable drugs have also widened the effectiveness of drug testing.

The Dublin Enquiry, established by the Canadian government following the Ben Johnson case, hinted that it considered drug abuse to be endemic in elite sport. Subsequent investigations implicated Johnson's coach, Charlie Francis and a medical adviser, Dr George Astaphan, who both seemed to have been taken in by Bulgarian claims that doctors in Sofia had discovered a way to foil the drug testers by using bridging periods and masking drugs. (Bridging periods are lengths of time before competitions during which the body flushes out any drugs. Masking drugs are natural hormones that hide the presence of illegal drugs.) Francis later confessed that thirteen of the male and female athletes he coached had taken steroids in their preparation for major championships.

The very fine line between what is legal and illegal creates dilemmas for both the performer and authorities. A sprinter can legally take ginseng, although it contains substances that have advantageous effects. Similarly, an athlete can train at high altitude to try to develop the efficiency of their vascular system, but blood doping itself is illegal.

A substance is only illegal if it is on the IOC list of banned substances. It is quite possible that athletes, coaches or others with access to highly qualified chemists and physiologists are able to keep one step ahead of testing procedures by taking substances which have not yet been banned.

The specific lists of banned substances vary from sport to sport, but those which are prohibited generally include:

- anabolic agents;
- amphetamines;
- corticosteroids;
- peptide hormones;
- stimulants;
- narcotic analgesics;
- beta blockers.

Blood transfusion and the use of certain drugs to mask the presence of illegal substances in the urine are also banned.

Drug-testing is now a huge industry which involves testing athletes at all levels of sport, both in and out of the competitive season. It is the random out-of-season testing that the sports authorities believe is the most effective means of controlling the problem.

The most common means of testing is by taking and analysing urine samples, although there are currently moves to increase the use of (more reliable) blood testing. There are, of course, certain health and ethical issues associated with the collecting of blood samples, and, as yet, sports authorities have not felt able to make this mandatory.

Any attempt to impede the detection of banned substances is in itself an offence, although some athletes have been known to introduce uncontaminated urine (supplied by a third party) into their bladder by means of catheterisation.

BOX 11.1 DRUGS TESTS AT THE OLYMPICS

'Six positive drug tests in an Olympics is not an epidemic' said IOC vice-president Dick Pound. 'If you read anywhere, or hear anywhere that these are the drug-tainted Olympics, that is just not so.'

On Sunday, hours before the Closing Ceremonies, the IOC announced two more drug positives, both for nandralone . . . that made it eight!

However, that does not include the forty-one would-be Olympians who were excluded before they ever reached Sydney. Another nine were thrown out after they got there – including Rumanian hammer thrower Mihaela Melinte, who was escorted from the track as she was about to compete.

CNN News, Sunday 1 October 2000

Twenty-seven of the athletes excluded before the games came from China, which had embarked on a long-term, tough and complicated crackdown. China is, after all, host to the games of 2008.

The drug-testing protocol used during competition involves the identification of a set number of performers to be tested. In athletic events, this usually includes all medal winners plus a number of other competitors. In a team sport such as soccer, it will normally include two randomly selected players from each team.

Two samples (labelled 'A' and 'B') are taken from each athlete and both are transported to an accredited laboratory. Initially, the 'A' sample is analysed, and only if this reveals any banned substance does the athlete in question have the right to ask for the second sample to be analysed as a confirmation of the findings.

Out-of-season testing utilises a similar process, with the key difference being that it is undertaken at the discretion of sports governing bodies in each country. It is simply too expensive for international bodies to carry out this type of testing as well as 'in-competition' testing.

Impartiality

Mars (1996) explains the potential risk that national sporting bodies may unofficially tip off an athlete of an impending out-of-season test. This may be done in order to avoid the associated bad press or to ensure the continued success of the athlete and, therefore, the nation. The process may be further complicated by the fact that many athletes currently spend their 'off season' out of their home country for warm-weather training or acclimatisation, which makes it difficult for national governing bodies to track and test their own athletes. Several major sports have sought to minimise this problem by handing over the task of out-of-season testing to independent companies with networks of sampling officers established around the world. However, there still appears to be a strong belief that the drug users are winning the war. Quite simply, the amount of money spent on drug development far outweighs the comparatively tiny amount spent by all sports authorities on testing. The speed with which new drugs and practices are developed also makes it very difficult for 'the good guys' to keep ahead of the game.

How 'legal' is it?

The other major dilemma facing the sports authorities in this era of 'open' sports is the legality of the whole process. If an athlete is banned from participating in their sport for two years, this means a loss of their main source of income. Many now consider that they have a legal right to challenge such a ban. The most notable case to date is probably that of 400-metre sprinter Harry 'Butch' Reynolds of the USA. Reynolds, an Olympics silver medallist, was banned from competition after a positive drugs test at the Monte Carlo Track and Field Grand Prix in August 1990. Reynolds challenged the ban, and the court found in his favour, awarding him 27 million dollars in lost earnings.

The counter-argument to the whole debate is that both audiences and sports entrepreneurs want to see improvements in performance. This will not happen without the aid of technology, which would include chemical supplements. Most elite athletes need to take supplements as part of their diet so that their bodies can cope with the physical demands of modern-day sport. A look in the classified section of any sports-specific magazine will reveal the variety and scope of dietary supplements available.

Implications

The Guardian of Saturday 23 October 2003 carried a piece highlighting the concerns of one of the major sponsors of track-and-field athletics over the issue of drugs in the sport generally and certain athletes particularly. The company, which signed a four-year £20 million sponsorship in 2002, was concerned about a number of issues in the sport. Whilst drug-testing procedures were considered to be satisfactorily in place and doping agencies doing their work properly, there was concern that athletes were getting caught.

The money put up by sponsors is considered crucial, not only for athletics but also for other sports too. In this specific context, the funding of a number of grass-roots schemes for emerging talent, the financing of travel and equipment for some elite athletes and equipment and specialist staff for other athletes would all have been at risk without the help of this particular sponsor.

As suggested above, there is a very narrow line between what is legal and what is illegal, what is acceptable and what isn't. There is the question of what is and what isn't sport, and such questions are raised in this and countless other texts. A very high level of entertainment is undeniably provided by many top-class sportsmen and women, but is it always sport, is it always fair and is it always legal?

So, that's OK then, is it?

We must therefore consider whether there are real dangers in allowing (or appearing to allow) a slow, creeping acceptance of a new sporting morality, whereby the medical profession, politicians, the media and sports themselves collude, almost by acquiescing, to change the moral and ethical basis on which sport has at least attempted to base its principles and justify its purpose. Is it simply a case of having given over our sports into the hands of the marketing professionals and the media barons we must now put up with whatever they are turned into?

WADA

The World Anti-Doping Agency (WADA) was established in November 1999 with the IOC playing a leading role in its formation. Thus far (2004), WADA has reached agreements with thirty-four international sports federations governing Olympic summer and winter sports to conduct unannounced, out-of-competition tests, and developed a harmonised universal anti-doping code. WADA still has concerns about sports outside of the Olympic movement (notably in the major leagues in the USA) that operate their own anti-doping policies, many of which are less stringent than those upheld by WADA.

1 Explain what is meant by the term 'performance-enhancing drug'.
2 Give four examples of the use of performance-enhancing drugs in a sport of your choice.
3 Explain who determines whether a drug is illegal in sport.
4 Discuss the incentives that may lead to an athlete taking drugs in order to improve their sporting performance.
5 What legal issues do sports authorities have to bear in mind when legislating upon drugs in sport?
6 Describe the testing process.
7 Why is random out-of-season testing seen to be more effective in drug control?
8 Discuss how drug-taking is the ultimate form of gamesmanship.
9 What argument can be put forward for legalising drugs in sport?
10 Can you suggest more effective forms of punishment for athletes found guilty of drug-taking?

Texts referred to in this chapter

Cashmore, E. (1996) *Making Sense of Sports*, 2nd edn, London and New York: Routledge.
Mars, M. (1996) 'Drugs and Drugs Testing', in D. Levinson and K. Christensen (eds), *Encyclopaedia of World Sport*, Oxford: ABC Clio.
Messner, M. (1992) *Power at Play*, Boston, Mass.: Beacon Press.
Scott, J. (1971) *The Athletic Revolution*, Glencoe, Ill.: Free Press.

chapter twelve

WHAT THE FUTURE HOLDS

> Sporting success depends upon having a structure in place that supports talented young performers every step of the way. Coaching, competition, facilities and support services need to be available at the appropriate level throughout the system not just at the elite end of sport. Creating a linked, progressive system of talent development is vital if we are to provide an opportunity for the very best to emerge.
>
> *DCMS (2001)*

Many factors have contributed to the improvements in sports performances in recent decades. Many nations are now following adaptations of the systems developed initially by East Germany and, more recently, Australia. There are great advances in research into techniques, technology, coaching, sports sciences and facilities, which are often made possible by the growth in the amount of funding governments have been willing to invest in sports excellence.

Finding the talent

A key development appears to have been in the field of talent identification. It has already been noted that Australia and now the UK are already utilising more scientific methods in attempting to identify sporting potential in the young. Governing bodies such as the EHA are unveiling grand plans in this connection and are currently working on a programme which will assess hockey players at under-fifteen, under-sixteen, under-seventeen and under-eighteen levels, after which selected players will be invited to development camps at regional centres of excellence.

Carefully structured approaches to talent identification are now becoming commonplace in many sports. The use of talent scouts has traditionally been the major means by which the pathway to sporting excellence has been opened. This process involves representatives from senior sporting organisations and clubs attending junior matches, camps and training sessions in order to 'spot' any likely talent – hopefully before any rival club or organisation.

Association football provides the best case study for the process in the UK, with a network of scouts watching literally thousands of games each week. The aim of a scout would be to identify performers with talent, an appropriately positive attitude and ideal physical characteristics. The 'identified' athlete would then be asked to join the club or organisation the scout represents. In professional sport, this may also include some form of contractual undertaking and receipt of payment in return for attending training sessions and playing. Until relatively recently, this traditional system relied solely on visual evidence and the objective assessment of talent alone. Today, the use of sophisticated testing and measurement to help determine potential would follow up any initial identification.

Turning to testing

Formal or scientific testing involves a series of tests to determine the physical and physiological potential of young athletes for a specific sport. These tests were initially developed by the eastern bloc countries but were taken to new levels by the AIS in the 1980s. It is envisaged that psychomotor and even psychological testing will be increasingly utilised and become even more sophisticated as scientists continue to develop expertise in this area as a result of the increasing amount of data they receive.

Some critics suggest that the pressure to win medals (and secure 'world-class' funding) has caused many sports to skew their own strategies/policies towards elite performance squads, leaving other areas of development under-resourced. In the UK, the funding of elite sport is already under pressure. The reliance on lottery funding means that long-term income will remain unpredictable and dependent on the public support through the sale of lottery tickets. Even though the system proved successful in the lead-up to Sydney 2000, by November 2002, the UK government announced that it was cutting elite sports funding by £21 million.

Building 'success'

The use of technology is already a key element in the development of elite sports performers. The level of input will increase and the use of computers and other technological aids will push performances higher. Already rugby and football teams in the UK are using video and computer technology to identify weaknesses in opponents' defence as the game is being played. More sinister than this are developments in the field of genetics where there is already talk of supplements being manufactured that will alter the genetic make-up of an athlete. Such developments might, for example, allow sprinters to take a supplement that would stimulate the growth of fast-twitch muscle fibres at a faster than normal rate or maybe even alter the genetically predisposed distribution of fast/slow-twitch fibres. Another element of genetic research likely to influence sport is that of cloning and 'genetic engineering' where it is thought that it may become possible to produce babies who are genetically superior in terms of their physical and sporting potential (see Plate 12.1).

PLATE 12.1 Will we soon see a pool full of human fish?

Photo: Photodisc

Cashmore (1996) argues that in a number of sports, technological developments have been so great that the sports themselves have become dangerous or they have undermined the very nature of the competition. Racing cars go ever faster and endanger the lives of those who drive them, and javelins can be thrown far enough to endanger officials, other competitors and spectators. Tennis players now hit the ball so hard that the sport itself is besieged with accusations of being 'boring' and 'predictable'. Tennis authorities have minimally curbed the big hitters by reducing the air pressure inside tennis balls by 5 per cent.

Sporting attitudes

Here in the UK, we need to re-examine our attitude to excellence in sport. We may well have undersold our success in global sport. In the UK government's *Review of Sport 2002*, the UK is apparently ranked third in the world in a survey of the whole range of sixty international sports in which it participates. However, if we look at the ten most popular sports in which the UK competes internationally (such as cricket, football, netball, rugby, etc.), we are in fact ranked tenth in the world. Whether this suggests that we do very well across a broad range of sports because in many cases we are competing against countries that prepare less well than we do is not clear; neither is it clear whether we do less well in the more popular sports because we prepare less well or we do not – as yet – identify potentially talented performers sufficiently well.

So, even though the UK has not won the football World Cup, the rugby World Cup or a tennis grand slam event during the past fifteen years, it has won a range of other world championships. However, it tends to be the 'blue chip' events by which success is judged, and this may explain why Australia and France are repeatedly referred to as 'best-practice' models. They have achieved success in these 'high-profile' sports. It seems, therefore, that although the UK performs well in a number of 'lower-profile' sports, our teams and individuals will continue to be perceived as under-achieving until they start to win the so-called major events.

We should now be able to identify aspects of sporting excellence and elite sports systems from other societies and implement them in the UK. Many of the systems we have discussed in earlier chapters offer effective and proven methods which could easily be adopted, and some of them, such as sports schools and institutes, are already being developed in the UK.

Introducing further sponsorship opportunities for our top athletes, either through an extension of the current lottery model or directly from central government, would allow our top performers to train harder and more effectively for their chosen sports. It is not, however, simply a question of transplanting practices from other cultures/societies. Sport reflects the society in which it exists, and the way sport is administered and developed should reflect and mirror the values and cultures of that specific society.

There are a number of cultural reasons/constraints as to why we in the UK may choose not to adopt elite sports practices from other cultures, or, indeed, why we may not actively pursue any full-blown excellence system.

'Government cannot and should not dictate. But Government can and should ensure that the opportunities are there for those who wish to seize them. That is what we will be striving to do.'

A Sporting Future for All, DCMS, 2001.

Historically, the UK is in the unique position of having invented most of the world's modern sports and championship models. We retain 'world status' in the major sports, and venues such as Wimbledon, Lords, St Andrews and the refurbished Wembley are regarded as the acknowledged 'homes' of their respective sports. However, because of this pedigree, we do in one sense feel the need to excel in these sports whilst, at the same time, the UK's record of international success in tennis, cricket, golf or football is hardly the stuff of legends.

In topographical terms, the UK has a very small land mass with as large a population as is reasonable. Although the population base exceeds that of many countries, it will never allow us to match the sports-participation pyramid of superpowers such as the USA and China (and, before too long, those of other Asian countries), who can select their elite squads from populations greatly outnumbering that of the UK.

In terms of ideology, the UK is also somewhat unique in its attitude to sport. Many countries take a very nationalistic approach and use sporting success as a 'shop window'. When elite teams and individuals compete, they do so for the honour and status of their nation. The UK considers that it already has a well-established position with a long history and considerable international prestige. The attitude to sport here tends to be patriotic rather than nationalistic.

Similarly, in the UK, as discussed in earlier chapters, most sports development has in the past been driven by a philosophy of recreation rather than winning. Many of our sporting heroes are 'triers' rather than champions. There exists, especially amongst the media in the UK, a view that winners tend to be arrogant, and this does not sit comfortably in our culture.

There are also socio-economic constraints. Most sport bodies in the UK (particularly the BOA) resolutely maintain their independence, which means that the state has very little input into elite sport. Although the introduction of lottery funding has certainly improved the preparation of the UK's elite athletes, many still rely on family support and hold down a full- or part-time job whilst preparing for competition.

This is further complicated by the tradition of autonomy of each of the four 'home' countries and whether teams compete as 'England', 'Northern Ireland', 'Scotland', 'Wales' or as teams representing the UK or Great Britain. As each 'home country' also has its share of lottery funding distributed by its own sports network, the system becomes very complex.

Sports governance

In the wider European/global context, sport also has to address its new status as a major business rather than simply a collection of recreations and pastimes. The world in which sport takes places has changed and will continue to change, as, therefore, must sport and the bodies that control it.

> 'Sports organisations can be the victim of their own success, if they do not keep pace with the political, economic and legal environment in which they act. This question has been especially relevant in Europe, where the autonomy of sports and the governing role of sports organisations have increasingly been challenged by various stakeholders, court decisions or legislation. Sporting rules and procedures are challenged before courts or international institutions and several rulings and decisions have shaken up the sporting community.'
>
> *Rogge (2001)*

In addressing issues associated with the attainment of excellence in sport, we should not overlook the political, social and economic environment in which sporting activity takes place. The Bosman ruling addressed aspects of contractual freedom for elite sports performers, but other aspects of the Single European Act now require, for example, that member countries recognise the right of all citizens

what the future holds

to participate in sport and provide facilities to encourage this. Clearly, the implications of this for the base of the participation pyramid can only be positive.

1 Explain the role of talent identification.
2 How can the funding of elite sports programmes affect other levels of sport?
3 What role does technology play in the development of modern elite sport programmes?
4 How could genetics become part of elite sports programmes in the future?
5 Why is it not possible for the UK simply to adopt successful elite sports programmes from other societies?
6 What historical factors may constrain the UK from developing an effective elite sports programme?
7 What geographical factors may limit the UK from developing an effective elite sports programme?
8 What ideological factors inhibit the UK in developing effective elite sports programmes?
9 What socio-economic factors constrain the UK in developing effective elite sports programmes?
10 Explain the difference between 'win' and 'recreational' ethics.

Texts referred to in this chapter

Cashmore, E. (1996) *Making Sense of Sports*, 2nd edn, London and New York: Routledge.
DCMS (2001) *A Sporting Future for All*, London: DCMS.
DCMS Strategy Unit (2002) 'Where We Are Now: The State of Sport Today', London: DCMS.
Physical Education Department, University of Birmingham (1956) *Britain in the World of Sport: An Examination of the Factors Involved in Participation in Competitive International Sport*, Birmingham: Physical Education Association for Great Britain and Northern Ireland.
Rogge, J. (2001) 'The European Olympic Committees, GIS Conference: The Rules of the Game, Governance in Sports: A challenge for the Future', Keynote address.

chapter thirteen

THE CURRENT VIEW

'In an Olympic final there is little physically to choose between the performers. Each one is strong, lean, supple and gifted. All have spent years getting to this point. The problem facing their minds and bodies is that only one of them can be crowned the winner.'

(Hemery 1991: v)

Funding: the dilemma

Although the Sydney Olympics were a success for the UK team (officially the best result for eighty years), many are still not happy with the infrastructure and support which are provided back home in the UK.

Greg White, Chairman of the BOA Athletes' Commission, conducted a post-Sydney survey of British Olympians and described his findings as a damning indictment of training facilities in Britain. His conclusion to the responses to the survey was that the gold medals won in Sydney by British athletes were won despite outside assistance rather than because of it. Of those athletes surveyed by White, 8 per cent felt that facilities in the UK had deteriorated since the Atlanta games of 1996. Fifty per cent of athletes said there had been no improvement, and this was despite the boost that had been given to sport by the National Lottery since 1998.

Income for individual athletes was also an issue. White concluded that though most athletes wished to dedicate themselves full-time to their sport, they are constrained by limited funds. Again, it would appear that the National Lottery has had little effect on athletes' income. Eighty per cent of the UK team said they would prefer to be full-time athletes but they could not afford it. The average yearly income for an Olympic British athlete was £16,700. This compares with the national average wage in the UK of £22,248. The majority of athletes returned from Sydney with debts of at least £4,000.

There were rumours that lottery funding to sport would be cut shortly after the Sydney Olympics, and this prompted many of the athletes to speak out and urge the government to re-consider its support for elite sport. Sydney gold medallists Steve Redgrave and Denise Lewis both commented in an article for the *Guardian* (2 October 2000). Redgrave believed that the time was right to build on the success story of Sydney and was alarmed by talk that funding was to be 'stream-lined': 'Rumour has it that the budget will be cut. If that does happen it would be a big mistake. Funding needs to be long-term. If we can do this at Sydney, we can do better in the future.'

What should we do to develop a more effective programme of sports excellence? There are two essential requirements. First, a large amount of money is required to fund such a programme. Today's elite performers require state-of-the-art facilities, equipment and clothing. In modern sport, the difference between winning and losing can be microseconds. Money also provides access to coaches with experience and expertise as well as the sports scientists who will give performers the edge in their particular sport.

The second and perhaps more urgent requirement is that the administration of any such system should be properly coordinated. At the moment, our sports system is very diverse at all levels; we need sports to come together to share aims and objectives for the overall benefit of sport in the UK. Whatever the system, it will, of course, be the hard work and dedication of the individual sports-men and women that provides the key ingredient. Hemery (1991) summarises, 'Sorry folks! In the pursuit of excellence, there is no substitute for hard work, in sport or any other area of endeavour. The process may be intense at times, but a consistent, step-by-step approach is what's needed. Needless to say, self discipline is required.'

It may be that the England Rugby team is showing the way forward. Ranked No. 1 in the world in 2003, they were undoubtedly the best-prepared international team in the UK. A glimpse at their summer training camp of 2003 in preparation for the World Cup of the autumn of that year may give a valuable insight into the preparatory requirements of a modern international team. Every day of the camp, held at an exclusive hotel in Bagshot, Surrey, began with a conditioning session at 7.30 a.m. The team had brought a whole suite of fitness equipment with them, and, under the guidance of conditioning coaches, each player in the forty-three-man squad worked through an individually tailored conditioning programme. The conditioning session concluded with a short spell with the visual-awareness coach where the squad had to react to a fusillade of tennis balls fired at them in order to sharpen reactions. This was followed by five minutes spent in special canvas tubs filled with iced water to cool off and hasten recovery.

Breakfast was followed by skills training under the guidance of a range of specialist coaches. This session included individual skills and team skills and concluded with time spent with the defensive coach. In the afternoon, the group review video extracts of forthcoming opposition put together by the team's own video analyst and receive information on how to acclimatise for the tournament in Australia. This information not only covers the more obvious topics such as the difference in temperature and humidity but also information about the effects that dew will have on the ball and the playing surfaces.

Nothing was left to chance. The coaching staff realised that every other team in the tournament was analysing every game that England had played and would attempt to predict the game plan the team would be using. So, the key was for the team to break normal practice.

To quote an Australian: 'If we do what we did for the last Games we will be nowhere, if we follow the best practice internationally we may just be competitive, but if we fill each day with initiative we will win medals' (Rob de Castella, Director, AIS, 1995).

Justifying the cost

Clearly, some sports and sports performers rely more heavily on public funding than others. Those sports with mass spectator followings might reasonably be expected to keep their own house in order and to fund their own programmes of excellence. However, the pursuit of excellence does have a cost, which is far more sustainable in some cultures than in others. In that sense, this question may produce a range of answers dependent upon where and of whom it is asked.

What return is gained from the millions invested in sports programmes (of excellence and otherwise), and does such a return justify the outlay? Clearly, if the pursuit of excellence is based at least in part on the development of policies of genuine mass participation, then some 'payback' is gained in terms of higher standards of public health as a result of higher levels of grass-roots participation. Such rewards (or returns on investment) would clearly be a justification in themselves, whether improved levels of participation contributed to excellence or not.

In the purely financial sense, however, it also helps to justify such expenditure if it can be shown that sport earns money in other ways than the inflated salaries of many of its participants. It seems that sport is indeed 'big business' (see Box 13.1) and, as in most businesses, excellence clearly brings its rewards.

With London being awarded the 2012 Olympic games, momentum to get elite sport in the UK on the right track has increased and, in light of this, February 2006 saw yet another reorganisation of elite sport in the UK with the transfer of high-performance sport responsibilities from Sport England and the other home sport councils to UK Sport. UK Sport now has 3.8% of the total funding allocated to the Lottery good causes – around £50 million a year, and 23% of the total sport allocation.

UK Sport now assumes full responsibility for all Olympic and Paralympic performance-related support in England, from the identification of talent right the way through to performing at the top level. The support for elite athletes was also rationalised, with three levels of programme.

UK Sport and BOA's aim for 2012 is to win more medals than ever before and climb the medal table to the highest position possible in both Olympic and Paralympics competition. In reality this means fourth in the Olympic medal table (presumably behind China, the USA and Russia) and second in the Paralympics. They project that such success will require Team GB winning 60 medals including 17 gold medals from a squad of 120 potential medallists.

In order to support this, UK Sport announced the awarding of an extra £63.5m to Olympic and Paralympic sports as a first step. Summer Olympic sports are to receive an extra £58.8m up to 2008 and summer Paralympic sports £6.5m, meaning that all Olympic sports other than football and tennis will receive at least £465,000 a year. UK Sport will 'review progress' after the 2008 Beijing Olympics before deciding how funds will be allocated in the four years up to 2012.

The money is part of the extra £300m that Chancellor Gordon Brown promised British sport in the run-up to London 2012 in his March 2006 Budget. A new UK School Games, designed to unearth future talent, was also unveiled.

BOX 13.1 THE ECONOMIC IMPACT OF SPORT IN ENGLAND

In the year 2000:

- 400,000 people were employed in sport-related activities in England.
- Sport generated nearly £10bn in 'value-added' in England alone.
- Sport-related employment provides households in England with £5.8bn in disposable income.
- Sport in England contributes £5.5bn to central government through taxes compared to £660m received in grants.
- Households in England spent almost £11.5bn on sport-related goods and activities.
- Of household spending, 2.8 per cent is sport-related.
- Sport-related investment in England in the year 2000 was approximately £870. Much of this was commercial investment (£499m) with local authorities investing around £208m. Government investment during the same period was just £7m.

Source: *The Value of the Sports Economy in England*,
Sport England, 2003.

REVIEW QUESTIONS

1 Outline the type of science support a modern elite athlete requires in preparation for global competition.
2 Why is being a full-time athlete crucial to elite sport preparation?
3 What elements do UK sports organisations still need to improve in order to develop an effective elite sports programme?
4 Is 'win-at-all-costs' now the only ethic relevant to twenty-first century sport?
5 Explain the importance of the planned participation pyramid in the development of an effective elite sports system.
6 Is it justifiable for a society to spend a disproportionate amount of money on elite sports programmes at the expense of grass-roots sport?

7 What part should the state play in the administration of elite sports systems?

8 How do you think the preparation of elite performers will develop over the next century?

9 What part do elite performers play in encouraging participation at the grass-roots level?

10 How would you run elite sport in the UK?

Texts referred to in this chapter

Hemery, D. (1991) *Sporting Excellence: What Makes a Champion*, London: Collins Willow.

White, G. (2003) *The Value of the Sports Economy in England*: A study on behalf of Sport England, Cambridge Econometrics, June 2003.

CONTACTS FOR FURTHER RESEARCH

British Olympic Association
Telephone: 020 8871 2677
Fax: 020 8871 9104
Web site: www.boa.org.uk

British Paralympic Association
Telephone: 020 7662 8882
Fax: 020 7662 8310
Web site: www.paralympics.org.uk

English Federation of Disability Sport
Web site: www.efds.co.uk

English Institute of Sport
Telephone: 020 7273 1500
Fax: 020 7383 5740
Web site: www.sportengland.org.uk

Lilleshall National Sports Centre/UKSI
Web site: www.lilleshall.co.uk

National Council for School Sport
Web site: www.schoolsport.freeserve.co.uk

National Mountain Centre
Web site: www.pyb.co.uk

Scottish Institute of Sport
Telephone: 0131 270 9100
Fax: 0131 270 9101
Web site: www.sportscotland.org.uk

Sports Coach UK
Telephone: 0113 274 4802
Fax: 0113 275 5019
Web site: www.sportscoachuk.org

Sports Institute Northern Ireland
Telephone: 028 9036 8295
Fax: 028 9036 6406
Web site: www.sportscouncil-ni.org.uk

The English Hockey Association
Web site: www.hockeyonline.co.uk

The National Water Sports Centre
Web site: www.nationalwatersports.co.uk

UK Sports Institute
Telephone: 020 7841 9500
Fax: 020 7841 8855
Web site: www.uksport.gov.uk

UKSI Cymru
Telephone: 029 2030 0500
Fax: 029 2030 0600
Web site: www.sports-council-wales.co.uk

Women's Sports Foundation
Web site: www.wsf.org.uk

Youth Sports Trust
Web site: www.youthsport.ne

INDEX